Critical reasoning and the art of argumentation

Critical reasoning and the art of argumentation

Revised edition

M E S van den Berg

UNIVERSITY OF SOUTH AFRICA, PRETORIA

© 2010 University of South Africa

Revised edition

ISBN 978-1-86888-597-8

Published by Unisa Press
University of South Africa
P O Box 392, 0003 UNISA

Graphic designer: Nozipho Noble
Editor: Jane Smith
Typesetting: Marlé Oelofse
Printer: Business Print

Contents

 **Preface**

Like the first edition, the purpose of this revised edition of *Critical reasoning and the art of argumentation* is to help you develop critical reasoning skills and improve your ability to reason well about problems you may encounter in everyday life. Developing and applying critical reasoning skills is globally recognised as a basic competency, like reading and writing. In Africa, as in the rest of the world, we are confronted with many social, political and moral issues, such as poverty, unemployment, violence and crime, corruption, health care, insider trading, HIV/AIDS, and end-of-life decisions. The ability to think critically is essential if we are to deal competently with any of these issues. Developing critical reasoning skills will help you to unearth false assumptions, uncover hypocrisy, expose stereotypes, and lay bare wrong-headed beliefs.

I encourage you to analyse and question those in authority, including your lecturers, and to critically question stereotypical ideas (including your own stereotypical ideas) and fundamentalist thinking. I also urge you to apply the critical reasoning skills and techniques that you acquire in this book to real-life contexts: your work situation, your home and family, interaction with your community, and your engagement with other fields of study, such as psychology, health care, development studies, public administration, political science, teacher education, social work, jurisprudence, and so on.

Although some of the text has been rewritten to improve the general organisation and layout, the subject matter itself has not changed. The main changes in this edition are the following:

1. More up-to-date examples have replaced outdated ones. Some new examples have been drawn from major sociopolitical events that have occurred in South Africa during the past few years, such as the Zuma trial, political conflict, race relations, and xenophobia. Other new examples have been based on events that have occurred in the rest of Africa and the world, such as the situation in Zimbabwe, political events in Darfur, the war in Afghanistan, and the change of administration in America.

2. Some old exercises have been replaced by new exercise items drawn from newspapers, advertisements, political speeches, literary works, the internet, and debates about xenophobic violence, crime, the death penalty, abortion, euthanasia, inequality and health care.

Chapter division

The tone of this book is informal and reader-friendly. Many examples and exercises are included to help you improve your ability to reason well and to avoid fallacious reasoning. Numerous activities that relate to a variety of experiences are also included that require you to do things on your own in order to practise your critical reasoning skills as you progress through the book. Feedback is given to most exercises to help you evaluate your responses and pace yourself.

The book is divided into eight parts:

1. *What is critical reasoning?* In chapter 1, I explain what critical reasoning is, discuss certain reasoning skills that underlie critical reasoning and explain the difference between critical reasoning and formal logic.

2. *Obstacles to clear thinking: preconceived ideas and fallacies.* Chapter 2 deals with preconceived ideas and a number of common faults (fallacies) in reasoning; I explain what they are and why they should be avoided.

3. *Working with arguments.* In chapter 3, I explain what an argument is, what a statement is, and what premises and conclusions are.

4. *How to analyse arguments.* Chapter 4 focuses on how to analyse arguments and the analysis of complex arguments; it provides useful guidelines for argument analysis.

5. *Definitions, counterexamples and counterarguments.* Chapter 5 examines several different types of definitions and I explain why definitions play a crucial role in the evaluation of arguments. The role of counterexamples and counterarguments is also discussed.

6. *Evaluating arguments.* Chapter 6 deals with the evaluation of arguments and I explain the difference between empirical, value, deductive and inductive arguments. Useful guidelines are also provided to enable you to distinguish between good and bad arguments.

7. *Applying your knowledge and skills to the evaluation of arguments.* In chapter 7, I encourage you to apply your knowledge and skills to the evaluation of arguments. I discuss five steps that can be used to evaluate arguments.

8. *Constructing arguments and writing argumentative essays.* Chapter 8 deals with constructing arguments and writing argumentative essays. Here I discuss different kinds of writing, provide some guidelines for constructing arguments, and give you the opportunity to apply the knowledge and skills you have gained in constructing arguments to writing argumentative essays. I end this text by encouraging you to further explore the path of critical self-reflection and self-discovery. Critical thinkers who think for themselves, rather than blindly following the instructions of an authoritarian and indoctrinating closed system, are the key role-players in a free and democratic society.

What is critical reasoning?

CHAPTER 1

What is the use of philosophy, if all it does is enable you to talk ... about some abstruse questions of logic, etc., and if it does not improve your thinking about the important questions of everyday life?

Ludwig Wittgenstein

Every day we are bombarded with arguments, arguments that are often based on fallacious reasoning with the aim of manipulating our thinking and behaviour. We encounter these arguments in our reading, on the radio, on television, via the internet and, of course, in advertisements.

However, the ever-increasing complexity of information technology, the perplexity of human interactions, the diversity of societies in South Africa and globally, and the demands of the workplace require people who can think critically and who can make informed decisions.

It is important to critically examine the way in which we judge, evaluate and act, because the decisions we make may have an important influence not only on defining, experiencing and presenting ourselves, but also on the way we perceive and influence other people, shape the world and touch the lives of others.

The aim of this chapter is to explain what critical reasoning is and to explore some basic critical reasoning competencies. We will unpack these critical reasoning competencies to emphasise the importance of critical self-reflection in our quest for clear thinking. We will begin to understand how societal values, preconceived ideas and cultural attitudes cloud our perceptions and attitudes and stand in the way of clear thinking.

1   Introduction to critical reasoning

Critical reasoning is not a new field of study – it is as old as philosophy itself. The history of the quest for wisdom and critical self-reflection goes back as far as the ancient Ifa (Yoruba) oral philosophy associated with Orunmila (c 4000 BC), the prophet of the Ifa religion and father of African philosophy; the pre-Socratic philosophers such as Thales (c 625–545 BC), Anaximander (c 610–547 BC), Pythagoras (c 578–510) and Heraclitus (c 540–480 BC); the ancient Indian philosophers such as Mahavira (born 599 BC) and Buddha (born 563 BC); the ancient Chinese philosophers such as Lao Tzu (c 600 BC) and Confucius (556–479 BC); and the Greek philosophers such as Socrates (470–399 BC), Plato (427–347 BC) and Aristotle (384–322 BC).

Orunmila expressed the path to wisdom in two maxims, 'know thyself' and 'as above so below'. Buddha believed the path to wisdom and truth to be 'insight into the causes of error results in the enlightenment of the self'. Confucius taught that the root of wisdom lies in sincerity of thought, which is attained through a critical investigation of things. Socrates never put his philosophical teachings into writing, but taught orally. His philosophical method consisted of a dialogue with the arguer. Socrates would critically question the basis of the arguer's knowledge and, in the process of critical inquiry, he would reveal the assumptions and preconceived ideas on which the arguer's knowledge claims were based. Socrates was sentenced to death for corrupting the youth of Athens. He respected the sentence, even though he could have escaped from jail on several occasions. He drank the fatal cup of hemlock, not because he thought that the sentence was justified, but because he was prepared to die for his belief in the pursuit of truth and wisdom through critical enquiry. For Socrates 'the unexamined life is not worth living'.

These are only a few examples from the long history of world philosophy where philosophers applied critical reasoning in their search for wisdom and justice. There are many more examples for you to explore. Let us get back, however, to our own epoch and consider a more recent example of a critical attitude towards things we take for granted. In his quest for truth and wisdom, Ludwig Wittgenstein, a leading analytical philosopher of the twentieth century, emphasises that the goal of philosophy is not knowledge, but understanding (wisdom). According to Wittgenstein it is not enough to convince someone of the truth; it is not enough to state it. Instead, one must find the path from error to truth. What Wittgenstein means is that, on our journeys to wisdom, we must first find the path leading us out of the fog – out of our fallacious reasoning (that is, reasoning based on unsubstantiated claims and wrong-headed beliefs), our misconceptions, prejudices and preconceived ideas. The path from error to truth, that is, the path out of the fog, is the pathway to critical reasoning.

Critical reasoning, therefore, goes beyond acquiring knowledge and reasoning skills. The ultimate goal of critical reasoning is to know (discern) how to apply knowledge and skills wisely. Furthermore, we need to understand that knowledge and skills are empty without wisdom. Being able to apply knowledge wisely requires a philosophical attitude characterised by thinking critically and constantly being in a state of critical self-reflection. Note that I use the terms 'critical reasoning' and 'critical thinking' interchangeably in this book. When I speak of 'critical reasoning', this implies 'critical thinking', and vice versa.

With these preliminary remarks in mind, let us pause for a moment and reflect upon the phrase 'critical reasoning'. The question we are here concerned about is, 'What is critical reasoning?'

Exercise

Drawing on your own context, experience and knowledge, write down a definition of 'critical reasoning'. Write down what you think, even if you have a limited idea – there is no right or wrong answers at this stage. Keep a record of your answers to the exercises that follow so that you can refer back to them as you progress through the book.

A basic search on the internet will reveal that there are several classic and recent definitions of critical reasoning. Below I give you my definition of critical reasoning. Bear in mind that this is not the only definition of critical reasoning.

Critical reasoning is active, reflective and informed thinking that involves the ability to deliberately and skilfully question, analyse, interpret and evaluate ideas and beliefs in the light of the reasons, or evidence, which support them.

Let us analyse this definition to draw out some of the basic skills, or competencies, that underlie critical reasoning. By defining critical reasoning as *active and reflective thinking*, we are saying that critical reasoning is essentially an active process and a reflective activity which involves us raising critical questions ourselves and thinking statements and ideas through for ourselves, rather than passively receiving information from someone else and gullibly accepting the ideas and beliefs of other people. We will call this competency the ability to *think for yourself*. We will discuss this component of critical reasoning in more detail in the section to follow.

By defining critical reasoning as *informed thinking*, I am contrasting it with the kind of thinking which is based on personal beliefs, ideas and perceptions that are not supported by evidence and well-substantiated reasons. An important feature of critical reasoning is to reflect critically on the implications of our beliefs and to give reasons or evidence in support of our beliefs and claims. We will call this critical reasoning competency the ability to *reason critically in an informed way*. We shall discuss this component of critical reasoning in more detail in the section to follow.

By saying that critical reasoning involves the ability to deliberately and skilfully question, analyse, interpret and evaluate ideas and beliefs, I am saying that the ability to reason critically requires certain reasoning skills, these being the ability to: (i) recognise problems; (ii) question assumptions, values and motives; (iii) analyse arguments; (iv) clarify and interpret data and ideas; (v) evaluate arguments; and (vi) judge the acceptability and soundness of claims. I believe that these skills can be developed and improved with practice. Acquiring and developing these reasoning skills are thus not limited to a person's intelligence, no matter how gifted or limited that may be. We shall discuss each of these points in detail in the course of this book and I will help you to develop these skills and improve your ability to reason well.

Before we continue with the third critical reasoning competency, which is embedded in our definition of critical reasoning, let us pause for a moment and consider how critical reasoning differs from formal logic. In the past many people have asked me what the difference is between critical reasoning and formal logic. My answer is as follows: the *similarity* between critical reasoning and formal logic is that both deal with argumentation and argument analysis. However, there are fundamental *differences* between the two. These differences have to do with scope and applicability.

Formal logic examines the formal structure of arguments in logical language (meaning formalising or symbolising ordinary words into a logical language) and it employs precise rules for testing the validity of arguments. *Critical reasoning*, on the other hand, explores the nature and function of arguments in natural language and is concerned with the art of argumentation rather than the formal theory of reasoning.

Critical reasoning includes more than studying the *structure* and *validity* of arguments in the sense that it reflects on the *quality, character* and *soundness* of arguments. It therefore has a much broader scope than formal logic. Whereas formal logic generally ignores the meaning of statements in natural language (everyday spoken language, whether it is English, Afrikaans, Zulu, Sotho, or Xhosa), critical reasoning takes into account the following:

- That statements (premises and conclusions) have meaning as statements and as courses of actions.

- That statements have an emotive side because arguments expressed in natural language are seldom impersonal and value-free. Values, attitudes, feelings, assumptions and preconceived ideas are embedded in natural language and these can easily influence our reasoning.

- The quality of argumentation. This includes the meaning and acceptability of arguments (not only their formal structure and its validity), being aware how prejudice can influence our reasoning, how to use observation skills, how to be aware of different points of view, how to evaluate arguments, how to be culturally sensitive, how to be aware of preconceived ideas, and problem-solving and decision-making.

The third competency our definition speaks about has to do with the ability to know *how to apply the critical reasoning skills* you have acquired *wisely* and responsibly. This means that you, as a critical thinker, need to reflect critically on your own biases, beliefs and prejudicial attitudes before you can adopt a critical attitude towards the ideas and beliefs of other people. Critical reasoning is not about 'trashing' other people's ideas, beliefs and arguments. Instead, critical reasoning requires you to be constructive and creative by weighing up different points of view, offering alternative solutions to problems, and considering other possibilities and options. Being able to apply knowledge wisely requires a philosophical attitude of *critical self-reflection*. We will discuss this in more detail in the section to follow.

Before you join me in a more detailed exploration of the basic critical reasoning competencies, take a moment to refer back to your initial response to the question, 'What is critical reasoning?'

Exercise

Did your definition include some of the aspects of critical reasoning we have discussed so far? If so, congratulations! If it did not, there is no need to worry. We have only just started our journey of critical reasoning. As you progress through this book, you will gain a clearer idea of what critical reasoning entails. At the end of this book I will ask you again to write down *your own* definition of critical reasoning.

2   Three basic critical reasoning competencies

2.1   Thinking for yourself

Reasoning or thinking is different from daydreaming, mere reflex actions, and mechanical activities such as brushing your teeth or replacing a light bulb. Thinking or reasoning is a higher-order mental activity that involves judgement and coherence. Reasoning is purposeful thinking; it is therefore goal-directed. For instance, analysing a complex philosophical text, or creating mind maps to capture the key aspects of critical reasoning are both acts of purposeful thinking.

Critical reasoning is, however, more than just purposeful thinking. To think critically means to *think for ourselves*. To think for ourselves involves a critical attitude of reflecting upon how we think in various areas of our lives. To think critically is to question the world and thus to engage critically with the possibilities and alternatives that the world offers.

When we follow the instructions of others thoughtlessly, accept the authority of others without question, or take things for granted, we are not thinking critically. To reason critically is to think for yourself by challenging authority and critically examining dogma, that is, unquestioned knowledge claims.

Think about the anti-apartheid struggle and how Chief Albert Luthuli and Nelson Mandela challenged the apartheid system in South Africa. They critically questioned the large number of apartheid laws, such as the Population Registration Act (1950), Prohibition of Mixed Marriages Act (1949), Immorality Amendment Act (1950), Group Areas Act (1950), Native Laws Amendment Act (1952), the Bantu Education Act (1953–1955), and the Pass laws. All these laws were meant to put apartheid, that is, the white domination of all other races, into practice. Certain critical thinkers spoke out against the oppressive system of white supremacy. One of them was a young black lawyer who was arrested after the Sharpeville massacre in 1960. His name was Nelson Mandela. Mandela not only played a major role in South Africa's history, but also became the first black president of South Africa and a global icon of racial harmony, justice and equity. Mandela did not passively and unquestioningly accept the ideas and beliefs of apartheid, but actively questioned those beliefs and values.

2.2   Informed reasoning

We said that to reason critically means to think for yourself. We explained that people who reason critically do not take things for granted; instead, they think for themselves and ask critical questions about the claims, beliefs and opinions of others. When people learn to think for themselves, they challenge repressive systems and oppressive governments. Challenging repressive systems and oppressive governments requires the critical examination and questioning of preconceived ideas and societal beliefs, as well as political amenities such as labelling, gender discrimination, racism, sexism, fascism, segregation, and religious fundamentalism.

Questioning ideas, arguments and the claims of authority critically is, however, not enough. Critical reasoning also involves offering *well-informed and reasoned alternatives*. We cannot, however, offer alternatives if we are unable to determine the difference between weak and strong arguments, between unsubstantiated claims and well-supported reasoning. Telling the difference between unsubstantiated opinions and well-informed opinions is an important first component in critical reasoning.

An *opinion* is a personal belief or an idea about the value, usefulness, meaning, and so on of a state of affairs in the world. Opinions are generally based on people's perceptions and are, therefore, relative to the speakers' own experience, feelings and state of mind. Opinions are often insufficiently supported, and are thus disputable. *An informed opinion,* however, is supported by reasons for the soundness or acceptability of claims we make. As critical thinkers, we should be prepared to set out the reasons for our opinions. When we offer sound reasons for our claims, we are engaging in critical argumentation. In chapter 6 we shall discuss the difference between weak and strong arguments in more detail.

2.3 Critical self-reflection

Being able to think for yourself, make your voice heard and offer well-informed and reasoned alternatives is *empowering*. As critical thinkers, you should be suspicious of the claims of dogma, authority, belief systems, policies and theories. The bravest thinkers are, however, those who question their own beliefs, preconceived ideas and biases. Our knowledge of the world, ourselves and others rests on our ability to reason, which directs us to seek justification for our beliefs and the beliefs of other people.

Critical reasoning, then, is concerned with deciding what to believe. In striving to reach this goal we use careful reasoning, observation and reflection to perceive problems, examine assumptions (beliefs and ideas that are taken for granted), and evaluate biases and prejudicial attitudes. Remember, however, that critical reasoning does not only involve a critical attitude towards the ideas and beliefs of other people, but also towards your own beliefs and biases. A crucial part of critical reasoning, then, involves *critical self-reflection*, that is, the ability to reflect critically on your own assumptions, and to critically evaluate your own prejudicial attitudes and biases. Critical debate is required to come to a greater understanding of how societal values, beliefs, preconceived ideas and cultural attitudes influence your perceptions of others and yourself, and fashion your understanding of the world.

Exercise

Express your opinion on one of the following controversial topics by writing two or three paragraphs on the issue:

1. (a) Affirmative action
   (b) The death penalty
   (c) Xenophobia
   (d) Same sex marriage
   (e) The differences between men and women
   (f) Democracy and the current South African political situation

2. Now consider the following questions:
   (a) Why do you hold this particular view?
   (b) If you should reflect critically on your own thinking, do you think your opinion harbours biases, preconceived ideas and stereotypes? Why do you say so?
   (c) Where do you think your biases and preconceived ideas come from?
   (d) Would you say that your opinion is based on well-informed reasons and evidence?

In summary

It is indeed a challenging undertaking to examine *our own* assumptions and preconceived ideas! However, in my opinion, the enterprise of critical self-reflection and self-discovery is liberating and rewarding in that it allows us to think for ourselves instead of being indoctrinated and manipulated by stereotypical beliefs. It is empowering to think clearly, to think for yourself, to defend your own ideas and insights based on informed reasoning and to arrive at your own independent conclusions. When you learn to think clearly you can make your voice heard.

In chapter 2 we will discuss the issue of preconceived ideas and societal assumptions in more detail and explore the ways in which preconceived ideas colour our reasoning and judgement. I will describe a number of common fallacies (faults) in reasoning and explain why they should be avoided. There are many ways in which our reasoning can go wrong. Becoming aware of how we often get things wrong is a first step towards understanding how to get things right.

Obstacles to clear thinking: Preconceived ideas and fallacies

CHAPTER 2

Arguments, like men, often are pretenders.

Plato

We engage in critical reasoning whenever we give reasons in support of our beliefs and claims. For example, if we claim that active involuntary euthanasia is morally and legally wrong then, if we want to engage in critical reasoning, we have to give reasons to support our claim. Here is another example: if we claim that reincarnation is true then, to engage in critical reasoning, we have to provide grounds for holding this belief. In fact, a large part of critical reasoning involves providing reasons or evidence for our claims and beliefs. The better the reasons and arguments we offer, the closer we come to showing that our claims are acceptable and the more likely we are to persuade our audience that our point of view is correct.

Often, though, we fail to do this or we are careless in our reasoning. We become lazy and do not reflect critically on the beliefs and ideas we hold, or we may allow ourselves to be persuaded by the fallacious reasoning and preconceived ideas of others.

The aim of this chapter is to help you become aware of how and why we go wrong when we reason. As critical thinkers, we need to develop our analytical skills to distinguish good reasoning from bad reasoning (not only in the arguments of others, but also in our own arguments), to reflect critically on issues, and to rethink our own position. In this chapter, we will first explore the obstacle of preconceived ideas and then discuss a number of common fallacies in reasoning.

1   Preconceived ideas

Preconceived ideas are societal *assumptions* that have a decisive influence on our thinking. Preconceived ideas pose obstacles to clear thinking, simply because preconceived ideas, by their very nature, are ideas that have not been subject to critical reflection.

Where do preconceived ideas come from? Preconceived ideas are imbedded in all cultures and get their power from social conditioning. We all grow up in societies where we inherit certain biased beliefs, values and attitudes from our parents, school teachers, religious affiliation, peer groups, and friends. The customs, norms, values and social institutions we grow up with have a crucial influence on our worldviews, that is, the way we see the world, other people and ourselves. As a result of all this, we are often unaware of the preconceived ideas we carry around and we take these biased ideas, perceptions and attitudes for granted. For example, if our parents live with the notion that children are a burden, women are inferior to men, and that nobody is trustworthy, then these ideas are eventually inculcated in our psychological and emotional framework. In other words, we become conditioned to think in the same way as our parents. This is what we call 'social conditioning'.

In our societies there are many preconceived ideas about race, class, inequality, religion, men and women, heterosexuals and homosexuals, labourers and professionals, children, people with disabilities, and societies that are different from our own.

A typical preconceived idea in South African society is the following:

AIDS is an evil, scandalous disease that threatens the social standing of our communities. The status of people who are HIV-positive must be kept secret to protect the social wellbeing of our communities. If it cannot be kept concealed, then the carrier of AIDS must be expelled from society or even eliminated.

This argument is fallacious because it is based on the false assumption that, if we keep silent about HIV-positive cases, AIDS will not affect the wellbeing of our communities. The reality of AIDS, however, is that it kills thousands of people and affects the lives of millions of people every year. AIDS has nothing to do with evil or with the social standing of communities. AIDS is not a social disease that will go away or be cured by keeping silent about it. It is a physical disease that not only kills people, but also has a devastating effect on the South African economy.

We can therefore conclude that the preconceived idea that AIDS is a social evil, bringing disgrace to our communities, is based on a false assumption about AIDS. It is an assumption that is supported by neither reasoned argument nor evidence.

We all have cognitive blind spots and we need to deal with these, because these blind spots are weaknesses that prevent us from seeing both sides of an issue, from considering alternatives to a problem, from making informed decisions and from acting out of a sense of justice. When we uncritically harbour preconceived ideas, we block our way to clear thinking and to acting justly. These blind spots within our own thought processes can be unhealthy, harmful and even destructive to ourselves and to other people. We therefore need to examine our cultural attitudes and social assumptions and critically decide whether they are useful or whether we should reject them.

As critical thinkers, we should not take anything for granted; instead, we must think for ourselves and ask critical questions about the assumptions, beliefs and opinions of others; we should also be alert to fallacious reasoning, which tries to persuade us into adopting positions that are not supported by reasoned argument and evidence.

Note, however, that not all preconceived ideas are false and present obstacles to clear thinking. Some preconceived ideas are useful. For example, when we get up each morning and get ready for another day at university or at the office, we do not reflect critically on our beliefs about the working condition of the brakes of our cars, whether our places of work still exist or whether we really exist. These assumptions are useful and allow us to live our lives meaningfully. It would be impossible to live our lives effectively without taking some beliefs for granted.

Preconceived ideas are obstacles only when they have an unsuitable and damaging impact on the way we and others conduct our lives. Some preconceived ideas can destroy lives and damage the wellbeing of others. Preconceived ideas about homosexuals, women, black people, people of Jewish origin and people who do not conform to a prescribed belief system have had devastating consequences throughout human history. Think about the Stonewall Riots in 1969 (sparked off by a group of gay people who fought against police violence and surveillance, societal discrimination and oppression) and the Harlem Renaissance in the 1920s (a literary movement among Afro-Americans to restore and reclaim the image of black people in America and globally), the Nazis, the apartheid regime, and so on. These are all examples of the power of preconceived ideas and ideologies – ideas and ideologies that proved destructive and unacceptable and that required serious critical reflection and social resistance before they could be changed.

Exercise

Study the following ideas and decide which ones you think are preconceived ideas and which ones are not:

(a) Women are too emotional.

(b) Men shouldn't cry.

(c) Jewish people are money-grabbers and therefore untrustworthy.

(d) The conventional nuclear family structure is better than any other kind of family.

(e) Women are better at rearing children than men.

(f) Hard work is always rewarded.

(g) Critical reasoning is the careful consideration of beliefs or supposed forms of knowledge on the basis of rationality.

(h) Heterosexuality is the norm.

(i) We are a multicultural society where all nations blend together like a rainbow.

(j) Children cannot tell the difference between fantasy and reality.

(k) Not all employees are on time for work every day.

(l) All human life is sacred.

(m) Whites are more privileged than black people.

Answers

All the statements in the list are based on preconceived ideas, except for statements (g) and (k). Statement (g) is not a preconceived idea, because it can be supported by reasoned argument, and is therefore justified. Statement (k) is not a preconceived idea, because evidence can be provided in its support.

The first step towards critical reasoning is to acknowledge and critically examine the set of preconceived ideas that we all carry with us as a result of our social conditioning and cultural backgrounds.

We have briefly looked at preconceived ideas and explained why they are obstacles to clear thinking. Let us now explore a number of fallacies and see how they can trick us – *if we are not aware* of the fundamental flaws in their 'reasoning' – into a position that is not, in fact, supported by reasoned argumentation.

2   Fallacies

A *fallacy* is a deceptive argument that attempts to persuade us, but contains a fundamental flaw in its reasoning. All fallacies are misleading arguments that try to persuade us to take positions that are not supported by evidence or reasoned argumentation.

Like good arguments, fallacies are persuasive. The difference between a good argument and a fallacy, however, is that a good argument persuades us in a *legitimate* way, while a fallacy does not. A *good argument*

- goes beyond simply presenting true premises and a conclusion;
- gives reasons in support of a claim and has a structure that enables us to see that the conclusion follows from the premises;
- provides reasons that are appropriately connected to what is being claimed – in other words, the reasons are relevant to the truth of the claim that is being made in the argument.

By contrast, a *fallacy* persuades us in an *illegitimate* way:

- It persuades us to accept its conclusion, but gives no reasons in support of its claim.
- It persuades us to accept its conclusion for reasons that are not related to its claim – for instance, an argument can be presented in such a way that our attention is distracted from a weak premise to premises that we want to accept.

Consider the following example: 'Africa. Love it or leave it.' Are these the only two choices? Note how the fallacy uses emotive language to distract us from the issue about whether or not these are the only alternatives.

Note that not all unsound or invalid arguments are fallacies. The *difference between a fallacy and an unsound argument* is that a fallacy, although deceitful, tempts us to be persuaded, whereas an unsound argument does not. For example, if someone tells you that you should either go to work or stay at home, and therefore you should do both, her argument is clearly unsound. You can see at a glance that this argument is unsound because the arguer contradicts herself. Clearly there is nothing in this argument that tempts us to be persuaded. This argument is not, therefore, a fallacy.

Now imagine that you are told the following: 'No one in Polokwane has been to New York. I have asked 1 000 students in Sovenga and none of them have been there.' This is not sound reasoning because the arguer is generalising in terms of a biased sample – but nonetheless it is possible that we could be persuaded by this argument. It is thus a fallacy. Do not make the mistake of thinking that everyone who offers a fallacious argument is deliberately trying to trick us – arguers may be deceived by their own blind spots and bad reasoning.

A fallacy is a mistake in reasoning: in a fallacy, the reasons advanced are irrelevant or inappropriate to the conclusion the reasons supposedly support. Fallacies can be more easily explained, understood and avoided when we divide them into categories according to what makes them persuasive.

In this chapter I will discuss and explain fourteen fallacies that can be divided conveniently into three categories: distraction fallacies, emotion fallacies, and structural fallacies.

Category 1: Distraction fallacies

An argument can trick you by distracting your attention away from the weak point of the argument. Alternatively, an argument can appear to be sound because it contains a false link to an argument that *is* sound (this is how a con artist distracts people's attention). I will discuss six *distraction fallacies*: slippery slope, straw man, begging the question, equivocation, complex question, and faulty analogy.

Category 2: Emotion fallacies

An argument can persuade you by confusing emotion with reason. Although emotion has a place in our thoughts and debates, emotion can be used by itself to persuade, with no argument to support it. As critical thinkers, we need to discern between the appropriate and inappropriate use of emotion in arguments. We will examine six *emotion fallacies*: *ad hominem* argument, false appeal to authority, appeal to force, appeal to the masses, false dilemma, and hasty generalisation.

Category 3: Structural fallacies

An argument can appear to be sound because it presents a counterfeit resemblance to the form or structure of a valid argument. We will discuss two *structural fallacies*: affirming the consequent and denying the antecedent.

2.1 Distraction fallacies

Distraction fallacies are fallacies that try to distract attention away from the weak point of an argument.

Slippery slope

A slippery slope argument entails *reasoning in a chain* with conditionals (*if* so, *then* something else), where at least one of the if–then premises is false or doubtful. In other words, the conclusion does not follow from the premises.

A typical slippery slope argument leads us from seemingly unimportant and obviously true first premises to exaggerated consequences in the conclusion. In a slippery slope argument, our attention is distracted by the terrible situation presented in the conclusion. We do not check whether all the steps down the slippery slope are connected, because our attention is distracted away from the weak premise right down to the bottom of the slope (hence the term 'slippery slope').

Consider the following passage:

> Direct slavery is as much the pivot of bourgeois industry as machinery, credits, etc. Without slavery you have no cotton; without cotton you have no modern industry. It is slavery that gave the colonies their value; it is the colonies that created world trade, and it is world trade that is the pre-condition of large-scale industry. Thus slavery is an economic category of the greatest importance. (Marx 1936:159)

In this passage, Karl Marx speaks out about the evil of slavery. However, this is a misleading argument and contains a fundamental flaw in reasoning. It is a slippery slope argument, because it tries to persuade us to accept its conclusion:

> 'Thus slavery is an economic category of the greatest importance.'

for reasons that are not relevant to its main claim.

In order to understand how and where Marx's argument fails, let us bracket and number the statements in the passage. In chapter 3 you will learn more about the bracket-and-number method.

> [Direct slavery is as much the pivot of bourgeois industry as machinery, credits, etc][1]. [Without slavery you have no cotton][2]; [without cotton you have no modern industry][3]. [It is slavery that gave the colonies their value][4]; [it is the colonies that created world trade][5], and [it is world trade that is the pre-condition of large-scale industry][6]. [Thus slavery is an economic category of the greatest importance][7].

In the passage, statement number 7 is the conclusion of the argument, while statements 1, 2, 3, 4, 5 and 6 serve as premises or reasons that are suppose to support the conclusion. However, on closer inspection, we notice that the premises do *not* support the conclusion. In fact, the argument is fallacious because it leads us down a slippery slope in the following way: if we are persuaded to accept that the first premise (statement number 1) of the argument is true and that this premise leads to the second premise (statement number 2) and the third premise (statement number 3) and that the fourth premise (statement number 4) leads to the fifth premise (statement number 5) and the sixth premise (statement number 6) (*which they do not because the premises are not connected*), then we are being tricked into accepting an unsupported and misleading conclusion (statement number 7).

Here are two more examples of a slippery slope fallacy:

Example 1

Have you ever heard of this! My daughter tells me she wants to keep a pair of male and female kittens. But heavens above, I will not allow it! If we get a pair of kittens, then soon they will breed and we will have a house full of cats. And then she will want more pets. And soon we will be bankrupt feeding all these animals. I am not going to spend my hard-earned money for her to turn my house into a farm. (Adapted from Teays 1996:197)

Example 2

Listen here, Reggie, if we support the legalization of dagga in Africa, next thing it will be the legalization of cocaine, then heroin and then LSD. I'm telling you, pretty soon the whole of Africa will be on hard drugs. So man, don't support legalizing dagga. (Adapted from Teays 1996:197)

These arguments are fallacious because they try to convince us of the truth of the conclusion, yet their premises are doubtful and unrelated to their outrageous conclusions.

Straw man

The term *straw man* refers to a scarecrow which is supposed to frighten off crows or other birds, but is in itself very feeble. The straw man fallacy consists of making the arguer's own position appear to be strong by making the opposing position appear to be outrageous, or weaker than it actually is.

A straw man fallacy distracts us by making the opposing view appear absurd. We can identify a straw man argument by looking for two false premises in the argument:

- the premise that inaccurately presents the opponent's view;
- the implicit premise that you must either support this untenable or unacceptable position or you must support the view taken by the arguer.

Notice that in this kind of fallacious reasoning *no other alternatives are offered.*

In a typical straw man fallacy the arguer knocks down an opponent's argument by misrepresenting the opponent's views. The arguer creates a false dilemma by imposing a choice between either the opponent's weakened position or the arguer's preferred alternative.

For example, suppose an arguer claims that there is a desperate need for a nationalised healthcare programme in South Africa to provide for the needs of the poor, because the poor cannot afford to contribute to medical aid funds, but they still have the right to basic healthcare treatment. A respondent says that a nationalised healthcare programme in South Africa is 'pointless, because the rich will take care of the needs of the poor'. Note that this is not what was claimed in the original argument. What was claimed in the original argument is that there is a need for a nationalised healthcare programme in South Africa. The reasons in support of this claim are that the poor cannot afford to contribute to medical aid funds and that the poor has the right to basic healthcare treatment. The opponent's response, i.e. that a nationalised healthcare programme in South Africa is pointless because the rich will take care of the poor, is irrelevant to the point made in the original argument. The respondent thus attacks a straw man, rather than the real issue.

Here are two more examples of a straw man fallacy:

Example 1

We need an effective and proactive armed response security system in this neighbourhood. Of course some of you sitting in this meeting today oppose this view, but you apparently think that the terrible crimes committed in this neighbourhood should not be controlled by armed response.

In this example the arguer makes his argument look strong by referring to a supposedly opposing view that is obviously absurd (those who oppose armed response security are indifferent to the fate of the victims of crime).

Example 2

Don't even think about his position. Opposing the death penalty means letting criminals walk away from crimes scot free and giving them the green light to murder and rape anyone they choose.

In this example of a straw man fallacy the arguer makes the argument look strong by referring to a supposedly opposing view that is obviously absurd (those who oppose the death penalty are indifferent to heinous crimes, such as murder and rape).

Notice that it is sometimes difficult to distinguish between a false dilemma (either-or) argument and a straw man argument. The easiest way to detect the difference between the two is to keep in mind that the choices in a false dilemma are not limited to viewpoints; the choices that are offered could involve actions to take, objects to select, or events to opt for. A straw man fallacy, however, not only presents a false either-or premise, but also *misrepresents* the opposing viewpoint.

Consider the following two examples. The first example is a *straw man fallacy*, while the second example is a *false dilemma*:

Example 1

We should adopt a policy of banning all guns in South Africa. There are of course those who oppose this view, but they don't think about the fact that many of the dreadful crimes in this country involve guns. Statistics, however, prove otherwise. (Adapted from Cederblom & Paulsen, 2001:159)

In this example the arguer makes his argument look strong by referring to a supposedly opposing view that is obviously absurd (those who oppose the banning of guns are indifferent to the fate of those who get shot).

Example 2

Either we ban all guns in South Africa, or we let crime run violently out of control.

Here the arguer maintains that there are only two alternatives, and one is obviously unacceptable (letting crime get completely out of control).

Begging the question (*petitio principii*)

The begging-the-question fallacy consists of circular reasoning, where the arguer takes for granted the truth of what he or she is trying to prove. The conclusion in this kind of argument follows from the premise in the trivial sense that it only re-states the premise in different words. Because of the restatement this kind of argument is called circular reasoning. At the end of a valid or sound argument, you will know more than you did at the beginning. But when someone commits a begging-the-question fallacy, the audience knows nothing more than they did at the start.

The begging-the-question fallacy consists of circular reasoning, where the arguer takes for granted the truth of what he or she is trying to prove. The conclusion in this kind of argument follows from the premise in the trivial sense that it only re-states the premise in different words. Because of the restatement this kind of argument is called circular reasoning. At the end of a valid or sound argument, you will know more than you did at the beginning. But when someone commits a begging-the-question fallacy, the audience knows nothing more than they did at the start.

For example:

Lecturers should get paid for writing study guides, because human beings deserve to get paid for writing study guides.

In this argument the speaker simply repeats the premise as the conclusion.

Here are two more examples of begging the question:

Example 1

I can prove to you that God is good. God has all virtues. Benevolence is a virtue. Therefore, God is benevolent. (Descartes 1986: 58)

Example 2

Margaret says that she is against the practice of affirmative action. She must be a racist. Therefore, she opposes affirmative action.

In these examples the arguments go nowhere and the arguers merely beg the original questions.

The begging-the-question fallacy occurs when what is supposedly proved by the conclusion of an argument is already assumed to be true in the premises. The purpose of premises in an argument is to establish and provide support for the claim contained in the conclusion. If a premise expresses the same proposition or statement as that of the conclusion, then that premise cannot establish or support the conclusion.

Equivocation

A fallacy based on equivocation occurs when a word or an expression shifts meaning from one premise to another. In other words, an equivocation fallacy is committed when a word is used first in one sense in one part of an argument and then in a different sense in another part of the same argument.

For example:

Insane people should not be punished. Anyone who murders must be insane. Thus murderers should not be punished, but treated in mental institutions.

In this example, equivocation occurs through the use of the word 'insane'. In the first premise ('insane people should not be punished'), the word 'insane' seems to refer to a person's inability to know right from wrong. In the second premise ('anyone who murders must be insane') 'insane' seems to refer to a person's inability to judge that what he does is cruel. In fact, it is possible that a person may know that what he is doing is cruel, but still choose to carry out the action anyway.

Let's look at two more examples where fallacies based on equivocation are committed:

Example 1

The average family in South Africa has an income of R5 000 a month. Peter has an average family, therefore Peter's family has an income of R5 000 a month.

In this example there is equivocation n the use of the word 'average'. The word 'average' in the first sentence means a statistical average (where all possible incomes are added and then the total is divided by the number of items), while in the second sentence 'average' means normal or standard.

Example 2

Because chocolate tastes good, it is good for everyone to eat chocolate.

In this statement, the word 'good' shifts its meaning from the first part of the statement to the second part of same statement. 'Good' in the first part of the statement refers to the sweet taste of chocolate, while 'good' in the second part means beneficial or healthy.

Words can mean different things in different contexts. As critical thinkers, we should be alert to fallacies based on equivocation, when a term is used in one sense in one part of an argument and then used in a different sense in another part of the same argument. Arguments based on equivocation are fallacious because their claims are misleading and/or ambiguous.

Complex question

A fallacy based on many questions (the complex-question fallacy) occurs when two or more questions are combined. The trick is to roll two or more questions into one question and then to demand a 'yes' or 'no' answer.

For example:

Have you stopped smoking marijuana?

Whether the person answers 'yes' or 'no' to this complex question, he is cornered. If he answers 'yes', he admits that he has been smoking marijuana. If he answers 'no', he admits that he is still smoking marijuana. The question: 'Have you stopped smoking marijuana?' hides an implicit question, namely, 'Do you smoke marijuana?' and cannot be answered without this implied question being answered as well.

Let us look at another example of a complex-question fallacy. Suppose an anti-abortionist asks an opponent the following:

Are you going to continue supporting measures that result in the murder of innocent children?

This question predetermines a particular answer, with the intention of winning the argument before any open debate or critical reasoning about the issue of abortion can take place. If a pro-choice activist answers 'yes' to this question, then it implies that he or she is in favour of the murder of innocent children. If he or she answers 'no', then the anti-abortionist could reply by saying, 'so when are you going to stop supporting measures that result in the murder of innocent children?'

Here is another example of a complex-question fallacy:

Is it affirmative action or the lack of work ethic that has brought about South Africa's economic distress?

In this example two questions are disguised as one question. A straightforward 'yes' or 'no' answer to this question would prejudice one's view in advance. The answer to the first question, 'Is it affirmative action that has brought about South Africa's economic distress?' may be 'no', while the answer to the second question, 'Is it the lack of work ethic that has brought about South Africa's economic distress?' may be 'yes'.

We must be on the lookout for complex questions because they close the door on critical and open debate. When you come across questions in arguments, consider how they are constructed to make sure that they do not determine a particular answer and so prevent critical debate.

Faulty analogy

The fallacy of faulty analogy occurs when a comparison is drawn between two different cases or issues, and there are no relevant similarities between them.

An analogy is made when the process of reasoning applied to one set of circumstances or characteristics is applied to another set that is, or seems, similar. The aim of an analogy is to explain a concept that belongs in one category by comparing it to another concept from a different category.

The value of a good analogy is that it makes a complex and abstract concept comprehensible and manageable by comparing it to something that is concrete and within the direct experience of everyone. A good analogy may also help us to see certain issues or points that are relevant to an argument in a new or different light. Using an analogy in an argument is an effective way of making one's point clear.

Here is an argument based on analogy where the arguer compares two entities and invites us to acknowledge some common features and arrive at a particular conclusion:

At Rogers and Rogers we are conducting an experiment to trace the causes of cancer. Since it is a well-known fact that mice and human beings share some significant genetic properties, we will take humans and mice as analogous cases with respect to certain diseases. It has been established that certain chemical substances cause cancer in mice. Thus, we conclude that the same chemical substances are likely to cause cancer in humans.

This argument by analogy succeeds because the similarities between the two entities are relevant, based on the grounds that mice and humans do share some significant genetic characteristics.

Note, however, that an argument by analogy only succeeds *when the analogy is suitable to the case.* If the analogy is unsuitable, the argument is based on a faulty analogy. A good way to test whether an analogy succeeds is to push it to its limits and to look at all aspects of the two things or cases being compared. Here is an example:

> A good woman is like a motorcar. She is under your control and makes your life a lot easier.

Is this analogy suitable to the case? Well, let us push it to its limits and establish the number of similarities (or dissimilarities) between the two things. Is a good woman similar to a motorcar? The arguer wants us to believe that they can both be controlled and can make life a lot easier. However, closer examination reveals that these apparent similarities are frivolous. Let us look at the differences between the two cases: a motorcar is a lifeless device and can be controlled. A woman is neither an inanimate object nor a device to be used for transport. A woman is a person and, like all persons, she is entitled to basic human rights. Unless she has been brainwashed or threatened, she cannot be controlled by anyone.

The analogy in this example is a false analogy because a comparison is drawn between two *different* things, and there are no *relevant* similarities between them, thus creating a false analogy. The strength of an analogy depends on the number of similarities between two cases or concepts, and the relevance of the similarities stated in the premises that lead to the conclusion. The key to identifying a false analogy is as follows: if there are no real similarities (or only trivial ones) and there are substantial dissimilarities, then the analogy cannot be said to be good or bad – instead, it is a false analogy.

In this section we have discussed a number of distraction fallacies. We explained that distraction fallacies can be persuasive because of their tendency to distract our attention away from the weak point of an argument. In the next section, I will examine six emotion fallacies.

2.2 Emotion fallacies

Emotion fallacies are fallacies that draw their persuasiveness from an illegitimate appeal to emotion. We say 'illegitimate appeal to emotion' because emotion fallacies confuse emotion with reason. Emotion fallacies are fallacies that provide a motive for belief rather than providing reasons in support of the belief.

Ad hominem arguments (*argumentum ad hominem*)

The fallacy of *argumentum ad hominem* occurs when, instead of tackling the issue at hand, someone makes a *personal attack on the character, circumstances, or interests of the person who is advancing a claim*, in an attempt to discredit him or her.

An *argumentum ad hominem* can work in a number of ways:

- First, it can be a personal attack that makes claims about certain *characteristics* of an individual that are almost impossible to change – age, height, weight, disability (blindness, epilepsy, paraplegia), gender, race, class, level of education or sexual orientation.

Here is an example of an *ad hominem* argument making a personal attack on an individual's character:

Dr Gumede is well known for his research and publications on sexual morality. But when he claims that sexual rights are human rights and that it is immoral, if not inhuman, to deny homosexuals sexual rights, he clearly doesn't know what he's talking about. Because, hey man, he is homosexual himself! Thus we can disregard everything he has to say about sexual morality.

This argument is based on an *ad hominem* fallacy, where the arguer makes an attack on an individual's person. The fact that Dr Gumede is homosexual is irrelevant to the issue of sexual morality and Dr Gumede's claim that sexual rights are human rights.

- Second, an *ad hominem* argument can be an attack that makes claims about an individual's *circumstances*. Instead of focusing on the reasons for accepting a conclusion, the arguer attempts to discredit a person because of his or her personal circumstances.

For example:

Mrs Msimang supports the proposal of a salary increase of 10 percent for senior members and 7.5 percent for junior members of the company. She argues that senior members have more responsibilities and work harder than junior members. But this is nonsense. She is a senior member of the company and, of course, she will support the proposal.

This argument is based on an *ad hominem* fallacy where the arguer makes an attack on the circumstances of the person who is advancing a claim. The fact that Mrs Msimang is a senior staff member is irrelevant to her argument in support of the proposal for salary increases. Seeking to discredit a person because of his or her circumstances has no place in reasoned argument. As critical thinkers, we must simply deliberate the reasons Mrs Msimang offers in support of her argument; her personal circumstances are totally irrelevant.

- A third common form of an *ad hominem* argument is to deny the claims of an opponent by focusing on the *interests* of the person who is making the claim.

Let us look at the following example:

> Mr Peterson endorses the proposal to move the Johannesburg Art Gallery from Joubert Park to Sandton. He argues that it will be in the best interests of art to move the Gallery and that moving the Gallery will make art more accessible to the public. Recently, numerous artworks were stolen from the Gallery, and Mr Peterson has a financial interest in the Gallery. So, of course, he is going to argue in favour of moving the Gallery to a suburb, where security measurement can be enforced.

This argument is fallacious because one cannot discredit an arguer's claim by exploiting his interests in the issue at hand. As critical thinkers, we are concerned with the soundness of an argument and not with the personal interests the arguer may have. The truth of Mr Peterson's claim should thus be considered independently of any personal and financial advantages he stands to gain.

To sum up, *ad hominem* arguments confuse emotion with reason. They concentrate on the character, circumstances or interests of the arguer, instead of focusing on the reason for accepting a particular conclusion. As critical thinkers, we must be aware of the *ad hominem* fallacy, whether it is an attack on the character, circumstances, or interests of the person advancing a claim. Critical thinkers are not concerned about attacking the person, but with focusing on the truth of an argument's premises and the validity of its construction.

False appeal to authority (*argumentum ad vericundiam*)

Argumentum ad vericundiam occurs when someone cites a famous person or authority to get a point accepted, rather than grounding their conclusion on solid evidence. What is important to note in all cases of false appeal to authority is that the 'authority' or 'expert' quoted is not an expert in the field under discussion.

Here are two examples of false appeal to authority:

Example 1

> The invasion of Iraq was justified. I know this because Admiral Palmer said so and he has been a combatant most of his life.

Example 2

> There is nothing wrong with subjecting animals to laboratory tests. Professor Williams is a nuclear physicist and in a recent radio interview she said that animal testing is fully justified in the name of human wellbeing.

What makes these arguments fallacious is that the authorities quoted are not credible experts in the topics under dispute. Although Admiral Palmer has been a soldier for most of his life, he is not an expert on the legal and moral justification of the invasion of Iraq. Likewise, although Professor Williams is a nuclear physicist, she is not an expert on the acceptability or otherwise of animal testing in laboratories.

When we quote an authority who is not an expert in the field under discussion, we are making a false appeal to authority. Note, however, that the authority of experts has its place and when we are constructing an argument we often appeal to the knowledge and insights of experts to support our claim. This in itself is acceptable, provided that the person or source cited is a legitimate authority in the area under discussion.

Appeal to force, or coercion (*argumentum ad baculum*)

The fallacy of *argumentum ad baculum* occurs when an arguer *appeals to the threat of force, coercion, or violence* in order to induce the acceptance of a conclusion.

Here is an example of an appeal-to-force fallacy, based on sexual harassment:

> Ms Radebe is due for a promotion and she has to go for an interview with her superior tomorrow. Her superior says the following: 'Ms Radebe, I would like you to come to my flat in Sunnyside tonight to discuss tomorrow's job promotion interviews. Meet me there at 8 pm and wear some sexy lingerie. Prove that you are worth it!'

The following is an example of appeal to coercion, where the arguer is using the threat of blackmail to persuade or force his opponent to his position:

> REGGIE: 'I don't believe that the ANC is the best political party to vote for.'
> BONGANI: 'Well Reggie, if you don't vote for the ANC in the coming election, I will tell your parents you have an illegitimate child!'

In the next example the arguer uses the threat of violence to persuade his opponent to his point of view:

> If you don't agree with me, I will break every bone in your body and you will land up in wards 1, 2, 3 and 4 of Ga-Rankuwa hospital, paralysed for life!

The appeal-to-force or coercion fallacy is often used by people in a position of authority and power, and it can be injurious to people's careers and damaging to their emotional wellbeing.

We should be aware of the appeal-to-force or coercion fallacy, where the arguer exploits emotion and fear in an attempt to persuade us into adopting a position that is contrary to what we believe in.

Appeal to the masses (*argumentum ad populum*)

> The fallacy of *argumentum ad populum* is characterised by an attempt *to persuade an audience based on popular feelings, mass sentiment or enthusiasm, or patriotism*, rather than offering relevant evidence or good reasons for accepting a conclusion.

Here are a few examples of this fallacy:

Example 1

Be cool, hip and trendy! Smoke marijuana. All the cool people do!

Example 2

LYDIA: 'Don't throw that coke tin out of the car window. That's messy! Our poor environment!'

GEORGE: 'What are you talking about? Everyone does it. Do you want to reform the whole world?'

Example 3

The majority of people hold the view that having children is a sign of wealth and status. So you should have more children.

Note that in the above examples no evidence or good reasons are provided for accepting the conclusion. Instead, the arguers appeal to sentiment and popular feeling to persuade us of their opinions. As in the fallacy based on an appeal to force, *appealing to the masses* confuses emotion with reason. We should be suspicious of 'arguments' that draw their persuasiveness from an illegitimate appeal to emotion instead of reason.

False dilemma ('excluded middle')

> The false-dilemma fallacy is also called *false dichotomy* or *excluded middle* because it involves the presentation of an either–or choice when, in fact, there are more alternatives.

One way of trying to make the world a manageable place is to categorise it into neat and exclusive packages. However, matters are usually much more complex and generally there are more than two alternatives to choose from.

Here are a few examples of the fallacy of false dilemma:

Example 1

Either we allow abortion or we force children into being raised by parents who do not want them.

Example 2

Either you support us in our cause to invade Iraq to investigate whether they are hiding weapons of mass destruction, or you are against our cause.

Example 3

Either you are in favour of socialism or you are a supporter of capitalist exploitation.

In these either–or statements the *complexity of the issues is ignored*. The false-dilemma fallacy rests on a confusion between negatives and opposites and excludes any middle ground. Either–or thinking is fallacious and an obstacle to clear thinking because it involves thinking in terms of either black or white, either for or against, either this or that, and ignores any gradations or consideration of alternatives.

In an argument we cannot always insist on negatives and opposites. The alternatives in many either-or arguments are not mutually exclusive. There can be many alternatives, not only two, and often we must allow for shades of grey.

Consider the following example in a divorce case:

Either it is Michael's fault or it is Irene's fault.

The unstated alternatives are that the fault may lie with both of them, or with neither of them. Perhaps they are incompatible, or maybe their parents interfered with their marriage; or perhaps the circumstances of their marriage were somehow flawed.

Hasty generalisation

> The fallacy of hasty generalisation occurs *when a generalisation is drawn on the basis of insufficient evidence.*

For example, Mr Thomson may infer that all chemical engineers are men, because he has not seen a female chemical engineer working in a plant. This is a hasty generalisation because Mr Thomson has not investigated all cases of engineers, male or female, working in chemical plants. Mr Thomson's conclusion may also be the result of a stereotyped and fallacious belief that gender is relevant to a career in chemical engineering.

The hasty-generalisation fallacy *often occurs in moral discourse* where a moral principle is drawn on the basis of insufficient evidence. Wanda Teays's definition of hasty generalisation is helpful here. Teays (2003:144) says that a hasty generalisation occurs when 'a generalisation or moral principle is drawn on the basis of too small a sample or an atypical case. Stereotypes and other poor inferences have been drawn about entire groups of people on the basis of either too little information or a group that is not representative'.

Consider the following example of a hasty generalisation, where a moral principle is drawn on insufficient and ill-considered evidence:

> Homosexuals cause AIDS, because we all know that gay men are promiscuous and HIV-positive.

This is a hasty generalisation, because a poor inference has been drawn about an entire group of people on the basis of insufficient information. Apart from the fact that this generalisation is based on a stereotype about homosexual people, the inference drawn is an incorrect generalisation. People often draw conclusions and make recommendations on the basis of ill-considered or insufficient evidence.

Here is another example of a hasty generalisation:

> Every Ford car I heard of is inferior and breaks down. My best friend drove a Ford for only six months when it started to give problems. My boss drives a Ford and his car is often at the garage to be fixed. So all Fords are inferior.

The arguer commits the fallacy of hasty generalisation because he jumps to a conclusion that is based on insufficient evidence. One simply cannot claim that all Ford cars are inferior based on only a few observations or occurrences.

Note that generalisations are not, in themselves, obstacles to clear thinking. Generalisations are acceptable and useful when inferences have been drawn from a general rule that applies to all cases, or on the basis of sufficient information or a smaller group that is representative of an entire group. *Hasty* generalisations, however, are obstacles to critical reasoning. When we evaluate arguments with premises based on generalisations, we should check whether they contain unfounded assumptions based on hasty generalisations.

2.3 Structural fallacies

Some arguments are unacceptable because of their *form or structure*. Structural fallacies *appear to be sound* because of a counterfeit resemblance to the form or structure of a valid argument.

In this section we will discuss two structural fallacies.

Affirming the consequent

Affirming the consequent fallacy is committed when the consequent in a conditional statement is affirmed and the antecedent is taken to be true on these grounds.

A conditional statement has the following form: 'If P then Q', where P and Q stand for statements.

For example:

If I left my wallet at home, I will not be able to pay for the groceries.

This is a conditional statement (P = I left my wallet at home; Q = I will not be able to pay for the groceries).

If it is indeed true that I left my wallet at home, then it follows logically that I cannot pay for the groceries. This is an argument with a valid structure, because the second statement or consequent (Q = I cannot pay for the groceries) is confirmed by the first statement or antecedent (P = I left my wallet at home).

An affirming-the-consequent *fallacy* is committed when the consequent in a conditional statement is affirmed on the grounds that the antecedent is true. Remember that, in an if–then sentence, the 'if' part is the antecedent and the 'then' part is the consequent.

Here is an example of such a fallacy:

If the economy is healthy, then unemployment is low. Unemployment is low. So the economy is healthy.

This argument is fallacious because there may be other reasons for low unemployment besides a healthy economy.

A fallacy based on affirmation of the consequent may be portrayed graphically in the following way:

1.   If P, then Q } P = Antecedent; Q = Consequent

2. Q
     $\therefore P$

Example

1.   If the economy is healthy, then unemployment is low. (If P [antecedent] then Q [consequent])

2.   Unemployment is low. (Q [consequent]. This premise affirms the consequent.)

Therefore: The economy is healthy. (P [antecedent])

There are many reasons why unemployment might be low (maybe unemployment was low as a result of job creation campaigns in spite of a poor economy), and the fact of its being low does not *logically or necessarily entail* the truth of the antecedent.

To illustrate this type of fallacy more clearly we will look at the following two arguments, one whose form is valid and one whose form is invalid:

Valid:	Invalid (fallacious):
Modus ponens	
Affirming the antecedent	**Affirming the consequent**
1. If P, then Q	1. If P, then Q
2. *P* $\therefore$ Q	2. *Q* $\therefore$ P

Example

1. If my car is out of petrol, then it won't start.	1. If my car is out of petrol, then it won't start.
2. My car is out of petrol. (This premise affirms the antecedent.)	2. My car won't start. (This premise affirms the consequent.)
Therefore: My car won't start.	Therefore: My car is out of petrol.

Notice that the argument on the right-hand side is fallacious because its form is invalid. It is an example of a fallacy based on affirming the consequent.

Denying the antecedent

Denying the antecedent fallacy occurs when someone argues that, because the antecedent does not happen, the consequent cannot happen. In a conditional statement it is fallacious to deny the antecedent and to assume that this is grounds for denying the consequent.

Here is an example of a fallacy involving the denial of the antecedent:

If it rains, the taxis will be delayed. It is not raining. Therefore, the taxis are not delayed.

This argument is fallacious because the fact that it is not raining does not necessarily mean that the taxis will not be delayed. The taxis might be late because of a boycott or a strike.

Remember that, in an if–then sentence, the 'if' part is the antecedent and the 'then' part is the consequent.

A fallacy based on denial of the antecedent may be portrayed graphically in the following way:

1.   If P, then Q } P = Antecedent; Q = Consequent

2.   *Not P*
     $\therefore$ Not Q

Example

1.   If it rains, the taxis will be delayed. (If P [antecedent], then Q [consequent])

2.   It is not raining. (Not P [antecedent]. This premise denies the antecedent.)

Therefore: The taxis are not delayed.

The fallacious reasoning comes in when the arguer claims that because one causal factor did not happen, the effect could not happen. There might be many reasons why the taxis are delayed, despite the fact that it is not raining.

As with the fallacy based on affirming the consequent, we can illustrate the fallacy based on denying the antecedent more clearly by comparing two arguments, one with a valid structure and one with an invalid structure:

Valid:	Invalid (fallacious):
Modus tollens	
Denying the consequent	**Denying the antecedent**
1. If P, then Q	1. If P, then Q

2.   *Not Q*
    ∴ Not Q
	2. *Not P*
	    ∴ Not Q

Example

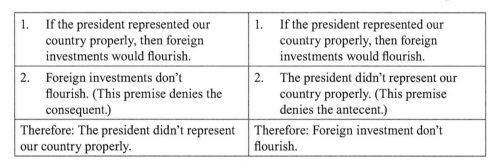

1. If the president represented our country properly, then foreign investments would flourish.	1. If the president represented our country properly, then foreign investments would flourish.
2. Foreign investments don't flourish. (This premise denies the consequent.)	2. The president didn't represent our country properly. (This premise denies the antecent.)
Therefore: The president didn't represent our country properly.	Therefore: Foreign investment don't flourish.

Note that the argument on the right-hand side is fallacious *because its form is invalid.* It is a fallacious argument because *it denies the antecedent.* There might be many reasons why foreign investments do not flourish, not just because the president has not represented the country properly.

The following exercise gives you the opportunity to apply the knowledge and competencies you have acquired in this chapter to a number of arguments. I have provided a summary of the fallacies discussed above to help you complete the exercise that follows.

Summary of fallacies

1. Distraction fallacies (distracting attention from the weak point of an argument)	
Slippery slope	Chain reasoning with conditionals (if so, then something else) where at least one of the if–then premises is false or doubtful and the conclusion does not follow.
Straw man	Making one's own position appear strong by ridiculing the opposition's argument.
Begging the question	Circular reasoning, where the arguer assumes the truth of what he wants to prove.
Equivocation	When a word or an expression shifts meaning from one premise to another (or from one context to another).
Complex question	A question where two or more questions are combined, demanding a 'yes' or 'no' answer.
Faulty analogy	A comparison between two different cases or issues, where there are no relevant similarities between the two.
2. Emotional fallacies (persuasion based on an illegitimate appeal to emotion – confusing emotion with reason)	
Ad hominem arguments (against the person or circumstantial)	Making a personal attack on the arguer's character, interests or circumstances in an attempt to discredit him or her, instead of addressing the argument he or she is putting forward.
False appeal to authority	Citing an authoritative or famous person who is not an expert in the field under discussion.
Appeal to force	Using force or coercion to force people to accept your point of view.
Appeal to the masses	Appealing to popular feelings, mass sentiment or patriotism to persuade someone.
False dilemma	The presentation of an either–or choice when, in fact, there are more alternatives.
Hasty generalisation	When a generalisation is drawn on the basis of ill-considered or insufficient evidence.
3. Structural fallacies (arguments that are faulty because their form or structure is not valid)	
Affirming the consequent	When the consequent in a conditional statement is affirmed and the antecedent is taken to be true on these grounds.
Denying the antecedent	Arguing that if something (the antecedent) doesn't happen, then something else (the consequent) cannot happen.

Exercise

Identify the fallacies in the following extracts and explain why they are fallacious:

1. Life is sacred and a gift of God. Taking the life of another person is a transgression of this principle. Euthanasia is the taking of another person's life. Therefore, euthanasia is the deliberate killing of another person.

    Why is this a *slippery slope* argument?

2. I could have told you that Mrs Thompson would argue in favour of salary increases for members of management. She is married to Prof Thompson, the vice-dean of Sciences, and she stands to gain financially by persuading members of the Board to increase salaries.

    What aspect of *ad hominem argumentation* is involved here?

3. 'I can prove to you that God is good. God has all the virtues. Benevolence is a virtue. Therefore, God is benevolent.' (Descartes 1986: 58)

    Explain how a fallacy based on *begging the question* is committed here.

4. You might as well stop trying to convince me that I must contribute to my father's wedding. I do not have money to waste. What is more, it is clear to me that his new wife will not contribute to sustaining the values of our community in Ulundi.

    Explain *equivocation* in this example.

5. We need an effective and proactive armed response security system in this neighbourhood. Of course, some of you sitting in this meeting today oppose this view, but you apparently think that the terrible crimes committed in this neighbourhood should not be controlled with armed response.

    Explain *straw man* argumentation and how it relates to the above example.

6. Most murderers are really mentally ill. I know this, because Judge Peterson said so.

    Here the arguer appeals to authority. Is it a legitimate source of authority? Explain the fallacy based on *false appeal to authority* by relating it to the example.

7. The Bible says God exists. Everything in the Bible is true, because it is the Word of God. Therefore, God exists.

    How would you explain this type of fallacy, characterised by *begging the question*, to your pastor or priest?

8. If John gets the promotion, then John will be happy. John is happy. Therefore, John got the promotion.

    Explain the fallacy based on *affirming the consequent* and relate it to this example.

9. You say that you believe in miracles such as landing on the moon and human cloning. If this is so, then I do not understand why you remain sceptical of the miracles narrated in the Bible. (Adapted from Cederblom & Paulsen, 2001:166)

    Fallacies based on *equivocation* take advantage of the different meanings of words. Which word is used in different ways in this argument?

10. Thousands of people hold the view that capital punishment is barbaric and has no place in civilised societies. So you should also hold this view.

    Explain why this fallacy is based on an *appeal to the masses.*

11. Statistics have shown that it takes three hours of uninterrupted rehearsal every day to turn a neophyte piano player into a professional pianist. So, if I practise playing the piano for three hours every day, I will soon be a professional.

    Explain the fallacy resulting from *hasty generalisation* and how it relates to this example.

12. Have you always been unreliable and careless?

    This seems like a *complex question.* Do you agree? Explain your answer.

13. You say that you are a socialist and yet you own a block of flats in Yeoville. It is impossible to be both a socialist and a capitalist. You are either for our socialist cause or you are against it.

    What is the main feature of a *false dilemma* as demonstrated by this example?

14. If he loves his children, he will get a job. He got a job. Therefore, he loves his children.

    Explain why this is fallacy is based on an *affirmation of the consequent.*

15. Don't believe everything Isabel says about the decisions taken by management. She is a woman and you know how they tend to overstate things.

    Explain how an *ad hominem* fallacy is being committed here.

16. If Samantha stars in the play *Waiting for Godot,* the play will be successful. Samantha didn't star in the play, so the play won't be successful.

    Explain why this is a fallacy based on *denial of the antecedent.*

17. Doctor Meinster, I hear you want to go to the media about that woman who died in Ward 5 as a result of neglect. Well, let me remind you of your malpractice case six months ago! You'd better keep away from the media or I will call the press about your misconduct!

    This is an *appeal to force*. What type of 'force' is involved?

18. You say that you do not support donations to cruelty against animals. I never realised that you were such an animal hater!

    The speaker is creating a *false dilemma*. In what way is he or she doing this?

19. Animals have souls. So you must treat animals the same way you would treat human beings.

    Is this argument going anywhere or is the speaker merely *begging the question*?

20. People are nothing but atoms. Any fool knows that atoms have no free will, right? So, people have no free will.

    This is both a *hasty generalisation* and a *faulty analogy*. Can you explain why?

21. We all have a right to possess a legally registered firearm. There has been a phenomenal increase in crime lately. We should be allowed to protect ourselves when our lives are threatened. Murderers and rapists carry illegal guns and they don't think twice before they shoot and kill. Therefore, we should be allowed to shoot and kill any trespasser on our private property.

    Beware when a speaker stacks up a number of facts and then ends off with 'Therefore ...' It may be a *slippery slope* argument full of pitfalls. Explain how this type of fallacy works in the example above.

22. Dr Nkosi, I hear you have called the press about the screw-up last week in the emergency room. You better keep a lid on this. Remember that I could tell the media about that nasty medical malpractice case you had last year!

    An *appeal to force* is used here. Explain why this is an appeal-to-force fallacy.

23. Digital computers and human beings are both physically complex systems that can process information. Digital computers do not experience pain. Therefore, the sensation of pain in human beings is not real, but imagined.

    Why is this a *faulty analogy*? What do digital computers have in common with human beings? Does the conclusion, 'the sensation of pain in human beings is imagined' follow from the premise, 'digital computers do not experience pain'?

24. Rosemary dated four engineers and they were all insensitive bullies. Therefore, all engineers are insensitive bullies.

    Explain how *hasty generalisation* is used here.

25. In a crime-ridden country like South Africa, the death penalty should be reinstated. Mr Ngobeni's argument against the death penalty is shortsighted. Opposing the death penalty implies that we as South African citizens consent to murder, rape, and other monstrous crimes.

    Why is this a *straw man* fallacy?

In summary

In this chapter we have dealt with the obstacle of preconceived ideas and examined a number of fallacies in reasoning. The point is not to only identify particular fallacies, but to develop a knack for recognising fallacious reasoning. You should try to apply the competencies you have acquired in this chapter to the evaluation of arguments (chapters 6 and 7) and the construction of arguments (chapter 8). When we learn to think critically and to write effectively, we need to realise that critical reasoning does not happen in a vacuum: we prove that we can think critically when we apply these skills in our everyday lives, at work, and in other areas.

Working with arguments

CHAPTER 3

Every man is encompassed by a cloud of comforting convictions, which move with him like flies on a summer day.

Bertrand Russell

Each and every day we encounter arguments in our reading, on the radio, on television and when we access the internet. We also, of course, encounter arguments in our conversations with others. In fact, we are flooded by an 'information overload', which includes many people trying to convince us about a variety of things: taking out a life policy, looking after a sick mother, not eating genetically modified food, joining in a strike for higher wages, voting for a particular political party, and so on. Often we are manipulated or confused by their arguments and, as a result, make bad decisions.

Critical reasoning can help you to reason well and to make informed decisions: it can help you to detect and avoid bad methods of reasoning, such as reasoning based on deception or the misuse of emotions. The aim of this chapter is to empower you to develop and sharpen your critical reasoning skills when analysing arguments.

1 What is an argument?

When we talk about an argument, we do not mean a quarrel between two friends or partners. In critical reasoning, when we talk about an argument, we mean the word in its philosophical sense. Because arguments have a central place in critical reasoning, it is important for you to understand what is meant by the term 'argument'. An argument is an attempt to convince someone that a claim (the conclusion) is true or acceptable. Here is a definition of an argument:

An *argument* is a collection of statements. One of these statements is the *conclusion*, whose truth or acceptability the argument tries to establish. The other statements are *premises* that are intended to support the conclusion, or to convince you that the conclusion is true or acceptable.

Note, however, that not every group of statements makes up an argument. In our definition of an argument we said that an argument is a collection of statements in which at least one statement (a premise) is offered as the reason for accepting another statement (the conclusion). The *premises* of an argument are supposed to lead to, or provide support for, the *conclusion*. The premises, however, do not always do so or are insufficient or weak. At other times, the argument may be poorly worded and may *assume* a common reference point that does not actually exist. Sometimes the argument may be missing certain pieces so that the picture is skewed and the argument biased.

To sum up, an argument is a group of statements. Some of these statements (the premises) are intended to establish the truth or acceptability of a claim (the conclusion), which is said to follow from these statements.

Exercise

Study the four claims (or points) that follow and draw up a list of six reasons (or 'becauses') in support of each claim:

Claim 1: The act of abortion is morally wrong.

Because:

1. It is the deliberate ending of potential life.
2. Every human being has a right to life.
3. Taking the life of a human being is morally wrong.
4. The act of abortion is psychologically harmful to the mother.

5. ....

6. ....

Fill in two more reasons or 'becauses' under 5 and 6 above.

Claim 2: We have a moral obligation not to destroy and pollute the environment.

Because:

1. Human life is crucially intertwined with the ecosystem as a whole.
2. Species are dying out on a daily basis.
3. If we destroy one part of the ecosystem, we may unwittingly trigger a chain of events that ultimately culminates in substantial detriment to human wellbeing.
4. The quality of air is getting worse and soon the earth's atmosphere will turn into a greenhouse.

5. ....

6. ....

Fill in two more reasons under 5 and 6 above.

Now, continue on your own and list at least six 'becauses' for Claim 3:

Claim 3: The death penalty should be reinstated to stop violent crimes.

Because:

1. ....

2. ....

3. ....

4. ....

5. ....

6. ....

Keep a record of your 'because' lists. In the next chapter we will return to them and construct arguments based on the reasons you have given for each claim.

2   What is a statement?

In the previous section we spoke about statements. But what do we mean by a 'statement'?

> A *statement* is an assertion that is either true or false. A statement makes a claim about some state of affairs in the world. If a statement asserts that a state of affairs holds, and it does, then that statement is true.

For example:

> The sentence 'Johannesburg is the capital city of Gauteng' is a statement. This statement is true because it asserts that a state of affairs holds, and indeed, Johannesburg is the capital city of Gauteng.

If a statement asserts something about a state of affairs, and it does not hold, then that statement is false. For example:

> The sentence 'Polokwane is the largest city in the world' is a statement. This statement is false because it asserts that a state of affairs holds which is not the case.

> *Note that questions, exclamations, requests and commands are not statements and they can be neither true nor false.*

> 'Is Johannesburg the capital city of Gauteng?' is not a statement, but a question. Likewise, exclamations, such as 'Oh great!' and 'Wow!' are used to express attitudes, but they are not statements and they do not have any truth value.

Also note: Although statements are expressed in sentences, we must *distinguish between statements and sentences*. A sentence is a group of words conveying meaning and does not necessarily claim something. For example, the sentence 'Well, gentlemen, there you have it' is not a statement, since it does not claim anything. It is not a statement because it does not have any truth value, that is, it does not assert a state of affairs in the world that is either true or false.

It is possible for one sentence to contain two or more statements. Consider the following example:

> The mother's right to life takes precedence over that of the unborn foetus because she has a concept of self, she is able to reason, she has the capacity to communicate, and she is a member of the moral community.

In the above sentence there are five statements. Let us identify each statement in the sentence separately. To identify the statements we will place them in brackets and then number each one in the order in which they appear.

[The mother's right to life has precedence over that of the unborn foetus][1] because [she has a concept of self][2], [she is able to reason][3], [she has the capacity to communicate][4], [she is a member of the moral community][5].

In chapter 4, when we explain the analysis of arguments, we will return to the method of bracketing and numbering statements.

Exercise

1. Study the following sentences and say which ones are statements. Give reasons for your answers.

    (a) 'The sleep of reason begets monsters.' (William Blake)

    (b) Please close the door behind you.

    (c) Great!

    (d) Is this an argument?

    (e) Abortion is morally wrong.

    (f) I wish I were rich.

    (g) All politicians are corrupt.

    (h) Why don't philosophers teach their children to reason well?

2. Read the following passages and indicate which are arguments:

    (a) The death penalty should not be brought back, because there is no evidence that it deters crime.

    (b) None of my grandchildren plays a musical instrument. Post-modern society must have stopped caring about music.

    (c) 'Marriage relations and the begetting and bringing up of children are far too important to be left to individuals and to chance. Therefore the marriages of the guardians must be regulated entirely by the state. The whole state will then be one family'. (Plato 1923:xxxviii)

    (d) Putting you in touch with the world. Connecting friends and family. That is Telkom!

    (e) He has been depressed since his wife left him.

    (f) If my car could fly, then there would be at least one car less on the highway.

Answers

1. (a) This is a statement because it asserts a state of affairs that is either true or false.

   (b) This is not a statement, but a request or a command (an imperative).

   (c) This is not a statement, but an exclamation.

   (d) This is not a statement, but a question.

   (e) This is a statement because it makes a claim which has truth value; it asserts a state of affairs in the world that is either true or false.

   (f) This is not a statement, but a wish or an expression of hope.

   (g) This is a statement.

   (h) This is not a statement, but a question.

2. (a) This is an argument because the premise, 'There is no evidence that it (the death penalty) deters crime' intends to serve as a reason for accepting the conclusion, 'The death penalty should not be brought back'.

   (b) This is not an argument. There are no statements in the sentence that intend to establish the truth of the claim.

   (c) This is an argument because a group of statements are given to establish the acceptability of the claim.

   (d) This is not an argument, but a group of utterances aimed at advertising and promoting Telkom. There are no statements in the sentence that intend to establish the truth of the claim.

   (e) This is not an argument because it does not claim anything. There are no statements that intend to establish the acceptability of a claim.

   (f) This is an argument. It is a valid deductive argument according to the argument's structure. However, it is not a sound deductive argument. In chapter 6 we will discuss the difference between valid and sound deductive arguments in detail. For now, you should note that the passage, 'If my car could fly, then there would be at least one car less on the highway' is an argument, even if the argument is quite ridiculous.

---

3   What are premises and conclusions?

We have noted what an argument is and we have explored the meaning of the concept 'statement'. Let us now explore what we mean by premises and conclusions. We can define a premise as follows:

> A *premise* is a statement in an argument that is supposed to lead to or serve as a *reason* for accepting the conclusion.

If we study the above definition of a premise closely, we notice that a premise has a specific function in an argument: it is supposed to give a reason in support of the conclusion of an argument.

The following example will help to explain the function of premises in an argument:

> Prisons in South Africa are an abysmal failure. First, they do not rehabilitate anyone. Second, they don't so much punish as provide free room and board. Third, they further alienate those with anti-social tendencies. Fourth, they bring criminals together, thereby allowing them to swop information and refine their offensive slyness. Finally, those who have spent time in prison are far more likely to commit additional crimes than those who have never been in prison.

We can bracket and number the statements in the argument to draw out the premises:

> [Prisons in South Africa are an abysmal failure][1]. First, [they do not rehabilitate anyone][2]. Second, [they don't so much punish as provide free room and board][3]. Third, [they further alienate those with anti-social tendencies][4]. Fourth, [they bring criminals together, thereby allowing them to swop information and refine their offensive slyness][5]. Finally, [those who have spent time in prison are far more likely to commit additional crimes than those who have never been in prison][6].

In our example, statements 2, 3, 4, 5 and 6 function as premises in the argument. Their function is to support the conclusion, 'Prisons in South Africa are an abysmal failure'. In other words, they provide reasons for accepting (or rejecting) the conclusion of the argument. In my opinion, the premises in the argument provide relevant and good reasons for accepting the conclusion of the argument. In chapters 6 and 7 we shall explore a number of criteria to determine whether the reasons offered in support of the conclusion are acceptable. For now it is sufficient to know that the function of premises in an argument is to support the conclusion.

Note, however, that it is not always the case that the premises in an argument support the conclusion. For example:

> I waited at the bus stop this morning. So, the bus will arrive.

The first statement of this argument is a premise and the second statement is the conclusion. In this case the premise does not support the conclusion. My waiting at the bus stop is not causally connected to the arrival of the bus. The premise, however, remains a premise even though it is false or irrelevant to the truth of the conclusion.

In some cases, arguments are incomplete. Sometimes authors present us with arguments that lack premises. We are then required to fill in the missing premises.

Look at the following example:

Alex is a bad manager because he spends all his time running his own private business.

In this argument there is a missing premise. The premise, 'He (Alex) spends all his time running his own private business', does not provide sufficient evidence or support for the conclusion, 'Alex is a bad manager'. We thus have to fill in the missing premise. Let us then rewrite this argument and fill in the missing premise:

> Managers who spend all their time running their own private businesses are bad managers. Alex spends all his time running his own private business. Thus, Alex is a bad manager.

The missing premise in the above argument is: 'Managers who spend all their time running their own private businesses are bad managers'.

Above we have explained what a premise is. Let us now define the concept of a conclusion:

> *A conclusion is a* statement in an argument that the premises are intended to support. The conclusion of an argument is also called the *point*, or *issue*, that is being debated.

Let us consider the following two examples and, in each case, identify the conclusion of the argument:

Example 1: An argument against affirmative action

> No one should be denied a job because of sex or skin colour. It's a simple matter of fairness that all people of good will should be able to agree on. That is what the civil rights movement was originally about. And that is what the feminist movement was originally all about. To discriminate against anyone on the basis of race or sex, white males included, is inherently unfair. (Adapted from Olen, Van Camp & Barry, 2005: 416)

Let us bracket and number the statements in this argument to draw out the conclusion:

> [No one should be denied a job because of sex or skin colour][1]. [It's a simple matter of fairness that all people of good will should be able to agree on][2]. [That is what the civil rights movement was originally about][3]. [And that is what the feminist movement was originally all about][4]. [To discriminate against anyone on the basis of race or sex, white males included, is inherently unfair][5].

The conclusion of the argument is statement 5, 'To discriminate against anyone on the basis of race or sex, white males included, is inherently unfair'.

The point the arguer is making is that all discrimination on the basis of race and sex is inherently unfair (statement number 5). The other statements in the argument (statements 1, 2, 3 and 4) serve as reasons for accepting this point, or conclusion, of the argument.

Example 2: An argument for abortion

Everything you say is based on a single assumption – that the fetus counts as much as or even more than the woman. But that can't be true. A woman is a full-fledged person. She has real desires and fears, real aspirations and memories. She's connected to the world through her family and friends. She cares about her life and her future. At the very most, a fetus has only the potential for all that. I'm not saying the fetus's potential counts for nothing. But what I am saying is that an actual full human life out in the world (the woman) has to count more than a potential full human life in the womb (the fetus). (Adapted from Olen, Van Camp & Barry, 2005: 128)

We can bracket and number the statements in the argument to draw out the conclusion:

[Everything you say is based on a single assumption – that the fetus counts as much as or even more than the woman][1]. [But that can't be true][2]. [A woman is a full-fledged person][3]. [She has real desires and fears, real aspirations and memories][4]. [She's connected to the world through her family and friends][5]. [She cares about her life and her future][6]. [At the very most, a fetus has only the potential for all that][7]. [I'm not saying the fetus's potential counts for nothing][8]. [But what I am saying is that an actual full human life out in the world (the woman) has to count more than a potential full human life in the womb (the fetus)][9].

The conclusion of the argument is statement 9, 'An actual full human life out in the world (the woman) has to count more than a potential full human life in the womb (the fetus)'.

The point the arguer is making is that (in the case of abortion) the woman counts more than the fetus (statement number 9). The other statements in the argument (statements 1, 2, 3, 4, 5, 6, 7 and 8) serve as reasons for accepting this point, or conclusion, of the argument.

Note, however, that sometimes authors may present us with arguments that lack a conclusion. In these cases the conclusion is *implied* and we have to fill in the missing conclusion. Consider the following example:

Restriction of the media is difficult to enforce. What is more, freedom of speech is a democratic right.

The argument seems unfinished because its conclusion is not given. We thus have to fill in the missing conclusion. Let us rewrite this argument and fill in the missing conclusion:

Restriction of the media is undesirable, because restriction of the media is difficult to enforce. What is more, freedom of speech is a democratic right.

The implied conclusion of the argument is: 'Restriction of the media is undesirable'.

In chapter 4 we will say more about implied conclusions and missing premises when we analyse arguments. For now you only need to note that authors sometimes present us with arguments that lack conclusions. At other times arguments are presented which lack premises. We are then required to fill in the missing conclusions or premises.

To summarise:

> *Premises* are those statements in an argument that have the function of supporting the conclusion. Premises therefore provide reasons for accepting the conclusion of an argument, although not all reasons that are given are good reasons or relevant reasons.

> *Conclusions* are those statements in an argument which the premises are intended to support. The purpose of an argument is to establish the truth or acceptability of the conclusion. A sound argument is one in which the conclusion is shown to be true or acceptable because it follows from the truth or acceptability of the premises and the valid structure of the argument.

Exercise

Identify the premises and conclusions in the following arguments. In each case, bracket and number the statements in the argument to draw out the premises and the conclusion:

1. The death penalty should not be brought back, because there is no evidence that it deters crime.

2. Affirmative action is fully justified. First, justice requires that we compensate for the results of past discrimination. Second, it is the only way to overcome racism and sexism. Third, affirmative action is a viable means through which the social ideals of equality and integration can be achieved.

3. If you are against affirmative action, then you are a racist.

4. Capital punishment deters crime. It saves the lives of innocent victims. It is a more powerful deterrent against crime than prison. And it keeps the convicted murderer from killing again.

5. The disclosure of confidential or privileged information by social workers without a client's consent could cause harm to the client. Social workers should protect the confidentiality of clients during legal proceedings to the extent permitted by law.

Answers

1. [The death penalty should not be brought back]¹, because [there is no evidence that it deters crime]².

    Conclusion – 1

    Premise – 2

2. [Affirmative action is fully justified]¹. First, [justice requires that we compensate for the results of past discrimination]². Second, [it is the only way to overcome racism and sexism]³. Third, [affirmative action is a viable means through which the social ideals of equality and integration can be achieved]⁴.

    Conclusion – 1

    Premises – 2, 3 and 4

3. [If you are against affirmative action]¹, then [you are a racist]².

    Conclusion – 2

    Premise – 1

4. [Capital punishment deters crime]¹. [It saves the lives of innocent victims]². [It is a more powerful deterrent against crime than prison]³. And [it keeps the convicted murderer from killing again]⁴.

    Conclusion – 1

    Premise – 2, 3 and 4

5. In this argument the conclusion is *implied*. Let us rewrite this argument so as to fill in the missing conclusion.

    The disclosure of confidential or privileged information by social workers without a client's consent could cause harm to the client. Social workers should protect the confidentiality of clients during legal proceedings to the extent permitted by law. *Thus social workers should not disclose confidential information without the client's consent.*

    The missing conclusion in this argument is: *Social workers should not disclose confidential information without the client's consent.*

    [The disclosure of confidential or privileged information by social workers without a client's consent could cause harm to the client]¹. [Social workers should protect the confidentiality of clients during legal proceedings to the extent permitted by law]². [*Thus social workers should not disclose confidential information without the client's consent*]³.

    Premises – 1 and 2

    Conclusion – 3

In summary

In this chapter we have defined an argument as a group of statements that intend to affirm the truth or acceptability of a claim. One of these statements is the *conclusion* of the argument. The other statements are *premises* that intend to lead to, or serve as reasons for, accepting the conclusion. In the next chapter we will explain the role of premises and conclusions in arguments in more detail and take a closer look at how to analyse arguments.

How to analyse arguments

If you think that your belief is based upon reason, you will support it by argument, rather than by persecution, and will abandon it if the argument goes against you.

Bertrand Russell

As critical thinkers, we should know how to analyse arguments clearly. This is because a complete analysis of an argument helps us to arrive at a better understanding of the meaning of the argument. The word 'analyse' means to dissect, or to lay bare. When we analyse an argument we want to lay bare the components of the argument. Differently put, we want to reveal the argument's structure. In order to do this, we should know how to identify premises and conclusions in arguments. This is often made easier by underlining the *signal words* in an argument. Signal words in an argument indicate which statements are premises and which statements are conclusions. In the first section of this chapter, I will explain the role of conclusion and premise indicators in arguments.

1   Identifying premises and conclusions

Arguers often supply signal words in their arguments that help us to identify their premises and conclusions. In the following example the person advancing the argument provides clues that help us to identify the *conclusion* of the argument:

> If private enterprise does better than the South African government at running businesses, then it will do better at running railway services. Private enterprise does better at running businesses. *We can conclude* that private enterprise will do better at running railway services.

In the example above the arguer tells us which statement is the conclusion of the argument: he or she uses the phrase 'we can conclude that'. Such phrases or expressions serve as clues to identify the conclusion of an argument and we call them *conclusion indicators*.

The following words and phrases usually signal conclusions:

Conclusion indicators		
therefore	consequently	as a consequence
in conclusion	this shows that	thus
so	accordingly	hence
it follows that	subsequently	then ...
we can conclude that		

Let us look at another example where the person offering an argument gives clues that identify the *premises* of the argument:

> *Since* smoking can harm those around us, we can conclude that there should be tight restrictions on the production of cigarettes. This is *because*, if smoking is harmful to those around us, then cigarette companies are manufacturing harmful substances; and *if* cigarette companies are manufacturing harmful substances, there should be tight restrictions on the production of cigarettes.

Here the arguer tells us which statements serve as the premises of the argument by using the signal words 'since', 'because', and 'if'. These words serve as clues to identify the premise(s) of the argument and we call them *premise indicators*.

The following words and phrases usually signal premises:

Premise indicators		
because	since	insofar as
for	for the reason that	firstly, secondly, thirdly, etc.
if ...	given that	seeing that
moreover	whereas	in the light of

Signal words in an argument indicate that the statement that follows is either a premise or a conclusion, depending on the indicator word.

> **Remember:** The statement that immediately follows a conclusion indicator is the conclusion. A statement following a premise indicator is a premise. This is easy to remember when you keep in mind that the purpose of premises is to give reasons in support of a conclusion, and that all premise indicators mean roughly *'for the reason that'*.

The purpose of analysing arguments is to reveal the *structure* of the argument. A useful way to establish the structure of an argument is to underline the signal words and so indicate which statements are premises and which statement(s) is (are) the conclusion(s). I will explain this method by giving two examples:

Example 1

Given that [all human beings should be treated equally][1] and *seeing that* [no person should be denied a job on the basis of race and sex][2], *it follows that* [job discrimination based on race and sex is unjust][3].

In this argument, the signal phrases 'given that' and 'seeing that' indicate that statements number 1 and 2 are the premises, while the signal phrase 'it follows that' signals that statement number 3 is the conclusion. This argument is an example of a *simple argument*, where there is only *one* conclusion.

Let us take another example of a *complex* or *chain argument*, where there is *more than one* conclusion.

Example 2

[We have a moral obligation not to pollute][1], *because* [ecology teaches us that human life is crucially intertwined with the ecosystem as a whole][2]. *If* [we destroy one part of the ecosystem][3], *then* [we may unwittingly trigger a chain of events that ultimately culminates in substantial detriment to human wellbeing][4]. *Hence*, [a serious regard for human welfare seems to necessitate our making every effort to preserve our natural environment][5].

In this argument, the signal words 'because' and 'if' indicate that statements number 2 and 3 are the premises, while the signal words 'then' and 'hence' indicate that statements number 4 and 5 are the conclusions of the argument. Here we have an example of a *complex* or *chain argument*, where there is *more than one* conclusion. There are three conclusions in this argument. The main conclusion is statement number 5. It is the main conclusion because this is the main point the arguer is making. The sub-conclusions in the argument are statements number 4 and 1. Did you spot all three sub-conclusions in the argument? If so, this is excellent. If you have marked only two sub-conclusions, you need not be too concerned about this. Analysing arguments takes a lot of practice. In the sections to follow you will have ample opportunities to apply your knowledge and competencies to the analysis of arguments.

In section 3 of this chapter, 'The structure of arguments', we will do a full analysis of arguments, using diagrams, to reveal their structures. Before we explore this, let us pause for a moment and do the following exercise:

Exercise

Question 1: Consider the following claim and do the exercises that follow:

The death penalty should be reinstated to stop violent crimes.

(a) Return to the 'because' lists you formulated in chapter 3 and arrange these lists to address the above claim in such a way that the strongest reason is at the top and the weakest reason is at the bottom of the list.

(b) Take the four strongest reasons and formulate an argument by using premise and conclusion indicator words. (I explained how to do this at the beginning of this chapter.) Always remember that the conclusion must be the issue that is being debated, or the main point the arguer is trying to make.

Answers

Question 1(a)

Let us assume that your 'because' list for the claim, 'The death penalty should be reinstated to stop violent crimes' consists of the following:

The death penalty should be reinstated to stop violent crimes, *because*:

1. The death penalty deters criminals from breaking the law.
2. Violent crime is rife in South Africa.
3. Some crimes, such as rape and murder, warrant harsh punishment.
4. The death penalty will alleviate the socioeconomic burden on the state to support violent criminals while they are in jail.
5. A significant number of the population expects the government to deal with violent criminals.
6. Violent criminals renounced their right to be protected by the state when they chose to disregard the law by committing the violent crimes that put them in prison.
7. The death penalty affirms the state's authority to protect its citizens.

Let us arrange our 'because' list for this claim so that the strongest 'because' or reason is at the top and the weakest reason is at the bottom of the list. We can rate our 'becauses' or premises as follows, where A stands for the strongest and G for the weakest reason:

1 = G
2 = A
3 = B
4 = E
5 = F
6 = C
7 = D

Let us arrange our 'because' list from the strongest premise to the weakest premise. The 'because' list now reads as follows:

2. Violent crime is rife in South Africa.

3. Some crimes, such as rape and murder, warrant harsh punishment.

6. Violent criminals renounced their right to be protected by the state when they chose to disregard the law by committing the violent crimes that put them in prison.

7. The death penalty affirms the state's authority to protect its citizens.

4. The death penalty will alleviate the socioeconomic burden on the state to support violent criminals while they are in jail.

5. A significant number of the population expects the government to deal with violent criminals.

6. The death penalty deters criminals from breaking the law.

The reason I asked you to arrange your 'because' list from the strongest reason to the weakest reason is to help you to formulate an argument. Note that this is an *exercise* to help you construct arguments. It does not mean that you have to agree with this claim. You can also use this method to construct an argument in which you argue against the death penalty.

Question 1(b)

Next, take the strongest four 'becauses' and construct an argument using the premise and conclusion signal words discussed earlier in this chapter.

The argument should now read:

Given the fact that violent crimes, such as rape and murder, are currently rife in South Africa, and *given that*, under certain circumstances, many of these crimes warrant the harshest form of punishment, namely the death penalty, *it follows that* the death penalty should be reinstated to stop violent crimes. *Because* violent criminals have renounced their right to protection from the state, this action seems deserved. The death penalty is further necessary *in the light of* the fact that it affirms the authority of the state to protect its citizens from violent criminals.

> **Note** that the conclusion of this argument appears in the middle of the argument.

The issue that is being debated, or the point of the argument, is: *the death penalty should be reinstated to stop violent crimes.*

Keep in mind that, even though the premises are supposed to support the conclusion, that is, the conclusion must follow from the premises, the conclusion does not need to appear at the end of the argument. The conclusion may be somewhere in the middle of an argument, as is the case in our example where the arguer makes the point that *the death penalty should be reinstated to stop violent crimes.* The conclusion in an argument could also be the first statement of the argument.

For example:

> Capital punishment is morally wrong. It is cruel and unworthy of a civilised society. Moreover, life imprisonment without the possibility of parole is sufficient punishment.

The conclusion in this argument is the first statement of the argument, 'Capital punishment is morally wrong'.

In the previous section I said that indicator words and phrases serve as markers to help us identify the premises and the conclusion of an argument. However, it would be a mistake to rely on indicator words only to identify premises and conclusions, since arguers often exclude indicator words because they assume that it is obvious which of their statements are premises and which statement is the conclusion. *What, then, do we do when there are no indicator words in arguments?*

2   Arguments without explicit indicator words

When there are no indicator words, it is more difficult to identify the premises and conclusions of an argument. Cederblom and Paulsen (2001:28) suggest that, in these cases, we should employ the *principle of charitable interpretation*. They define this principle as follows:

> The *principle of charitable interpretation* entails that, when more than one interpretation of an argument is possible, the argument should be interpreted so that the premises provide the strongest support for the conclusion.

Argument analysis is not a mechanical process; it requires *understanding* what you read and what the point of the argument is. Therefore, when you are dealing with arguments where indicator words have been omitted, you need to read the argument especially carefully to identify the premises and conclusion.

The intention of the principle of charitable interpretation is *not* to see where you can pick holes in an opponent's argument and to dismiss the argument just because its premises or conclusion are not explicitly stated. Rather, the principle of charitable interpretation entails reaching a decision about what is the *most reasonable* way of interpreting the argument. Arguments should be interpreted as if they were constructed logically, that is, in such a way that the premises give the strongest possible support for the conclusion. Applying the principle of charitable interpretation to identifying the premises and conclusion in arguments where there are no indicator words involves trying out each statement in the argument in the role of conclusion, with the remaining statements acting as premises. The statement that is best supported by the other statements should be regarded as the conclusion (Cederblom & Paulsen 2001:28).

Let us use the principle of charitable interpretation to identify the premises and the conclusion in the following argument:

> People who kill others do not deserve to live themselves. Such people should be treated as they treat others. Capital punishment is fully justified for murderers. The practice of capital punishment will make villains think twice before they act.

There are no signal words or phrases in this argument and it is not clear what the point of the argument is. Does the argument claim that people who kill don't deserve to live, or does the argument claim that capital punishment is justified for murderers? By employing the principle of charitable interpretation, that is, by reading each statement as if it were the conclusion, we can see that the third statement is the one best supported by the remaining statements. The *point* of this argument is that capital punishment is fully justified for murderers. The remaining statements serve as support for this point or conclusion of the argument.

Another way to identify the conclusion and premises of an argument when there are no premise and conclusion indicator words is to rewrite (interpret) the argument and fill in the missing indicator words. Let us rewrite the above argument to identify its conclusion and premises:

> *Since* people who kill others do not deserve to live themselves, *it follows that* capital punishment is fully justified for murderers. *Moreover*, such people should be treated as they treat others. *Furthermore*, the practice of capital punishment will make villains think twice before they act.

Exercise

Identify the premises and conclusions in the following arguments by filling in the missing premise and conclusion indicator words:

1. Either the government should protect children from abuse and neglect by their parents, or it should build more orphanages. The government will not protect children from abuse and neglect by their parents. The government should build more orphanages. (Adapted from Cederblom & Paulsen 2001:30)

2. Humans have been taking from nature for centuries without giving anything back. We've destroyed entire species, turned forests into wasteland, ruined water and air, turned soil infertile, and defaced our land to get at the resources beneath it. It is time that we stop inflicting senseless damage on nature. (Adapted from Olen & Barry 1999:458)

3. The killing of human beings should never be permitted by society. Capital punishment entails killing human beings. Capital punishment should not be permitted.

4. Smoking can harm those around us. Cigarette companies are manufacturing harmful substances. There should be tight restrictions on the production of cigarettes.

Answers

I will supply you with answers to exercise (1). Apply the competencies you have gained from the previous exercises and complete exercises (2), (3) and (4) on your own.

1. Either the government should protect children from abuse and neglect by their parents, or it should build more orphanages. The government will not protect children from abuse and neglect by their parents. The government should build more orphanages.

This argument does not contain premise or conclusion indicators. We therefore need to read the argument carefully to identify the premises and conclusion. By trying out each statement in the argument in the role of the conclusion, we can see that the last statement is the one best supported by the remaining statements. The *point* of this argument is that the government should build more orphanages.

We can rewrite the argument in the following way to draw out the conclusion and premises:

The government should protect children from abuse and neglect by their parents. *If* the government cannot protect children from abuse and neglect by their parents, *then* they should build more orphanages. The government will not protect children from abuse and neglect by their parents. *Therefore*, the government should build more orphanages.

3   The structure of arguments

In chapter 3 we gave a definition of an argument. Can you still remember it? We said that an argument is a collection of statements. One of these statements is the conclusion. The other statements are premises that are intended to support the conclusion. The basic components of an argument are, of course, its premises and conclusion(s). Earlier on in this chapter we said that the purpose of argument analysis is to reveal the structure of arguments. We have analysed a number of arguments which involved identifying their premises and conclusion(s) using the technique of underlining the premise and conclusion indicators. We have also employed the principle of charitable interpretation in cases where there are no premise and conclusion indicators. In this section we will do a complete analysis of arguments, using diagrams, to reveal the structures of arguments. The purpose of doing a complete analysis of an argument is to establish how an argument's premises and conclusion(s) are related. Differently put, a complete analysis reveals how the conclusion is supported by the premises. Premises and conclusions are connected in different ways in various arguments.

When we examine the structure of an argument, the first logical step is to identify the *conclusion*, that is, the issue that is being debated, or the point that is being made in the argument. The next step is to determine the *premises* of the argument. Then we have to decide how the premises are related to the conclusion. Here we have to ask ourselves how the premises support the conclusion. Do the premises support the conclusion *independently*, or do they support the conclusion *interdependently*? The following two examples show the difference between the two:

Example 1

> Active voluntary euthanasia upholds the rights of a terminally ill patient to decide whether to end his or her own life. Moreover, it prevents pointless suffering and torment. Therefore, active voluntary euthanasia should be legal.

We first need to bracket and number the statements in the above argument to identify the premises and conclusion and then determine how the premises support the conclusion:

> [Active voluntary euthanasia upholds the rights of a terminally ill patient to decide about her own life]¹. Moreover, [it prevents pointless suffering and torment]². *Therefore*, [active voluntary euthanasia should be legal]³.

Conclusion – 3
Premises – 1, 2

In this argument, premise 1 and premise 2 support the conclusion individually, that is, they support the conclusion independently of each other. If premises 1 and 2 are true, they *each* provide us with a good reason for accepting the conclusion. The structure of the argument can be presented as follows:

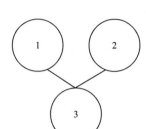

The diagram shows that premises 1 and 2 support the conclusion (3) *independently*.

Now look at the following argument, where the premises support the conclusion *interdependently*:

Example 2:

All persons have a right to life. Seema is a person. Therefore, Seema has a right to life.

Let us bracket and number the statements of this argument to decide how the premises support the conclusion:

[All persons have a right to life]¹. [Seema is a person]². *Therefore*, [Seema has a right to life]³.

Conclusion — 3
Premises — 1, 2

Here premise 1 and premise 2 support the conclusion *interdependently*. Both premise 1 and 2 need to be true, because they support the conclusion *together*. Note that neither premise 1 nor premise 2 *on its own* provides sufficient reason to accept the conclusion.

The structure of this argument can be presented as follows:

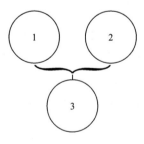

The diagram shows that premises 1 and 2 support the conclusion (3) interdependently.

> **Tip:** There is an easy way to check whether premises support the conclusion independently, or interdependently. Delete one of the premises in the argument and then determine if the remaining premise(s) support(s) the conclusion. If the remaining premises support the conclusion, then the premises support the conclusion *independently*. On the other hand, if you delete one of the premises and the remaining premise(s) do(es) not conclusively support the conclusion, then all the premises support the conclusion *interdependently*.

Now return to our first example, the argument for active voluntary euthanasia. If we delete premise 1 of the argument, which claims that 'Active voluntary euthanasia upholds the rights of a terminally ill patient to decide whether to end his or her own life', then premise 2, which claims that 'It [active voluntary euthanasia] prevents pointless suffering and torment' still supports the conclusion *independently*. But if we take our second example and delete premise 1, 'All persons have a right to life', then premise 2, which states that 'Seema is a person' does not support the conclusion independently, because it needs premise 1 to support the conclusion. Thus, premises 1 and 2 support the conclusion *interdependently*.

Remember that, in chapter 3 we said that some arguments contain missing premises while others have implicit conclusions. Sometimes arguments are presented with all their premises, but the conclusion is missing. In these cases, the arguer expects the context to make the conclusion clear and we are left to draw our own conclusion. For example:

[Abortion is the deliberate ending of life][1]. *What is more* [every human creature has a right to life][2].

The implied conclusion in this argument is that abortion is morally wrong. The structure of this argument can be illustrated as follows:

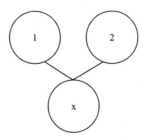

The diagram shows that there is a *missing conclusion*, namely X. From the context of the argument we have drawn our own conclusion, namely 'Abortion is morally wrong'. Note that premises 1 and 2 support the conclusion independently.

At other times arguments are presented with their conclusions, but some of the premises are missing. In these cases the arguer expects us to fill in the missing premises, which are necessary to affirm the acceptability of the conclusion. The missing premises are sometimes referred to as *assumptions*: these are views or positions that are likely to be held by the arguer, but not explicitly stated. Consider the following example:

> [Mike is a concerned father]¹ and he is *therefore*
> [opposed to his children staying out late at night]².

The missing premise is that all concerned fathers are opposed to their children staying out late at night. The structure of this argument can be illustrated as follows:

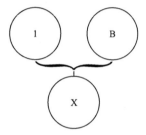

The diagram shows that there is a *missing premise* B. Above we have filled in the missing premise, namely 'All concerned fathers are opposed to their children staying out late at night'. Premise B is necessary to give sufficient support for the conclusion X. Note that premises 1 and B support the conclusion X interdependently.

Exercise

Read the following arguments carefully and then fill in the missing premises and conclusions. Draw a diagram in each case to reveal the argument's structure and establish how the argument's premises and conclusion(s) are related.

1. A law that bans the use of marijuana is a bad idea, because anything that would put ordinary social marijuana smokers in jail is a bad idea.

2. Noise is a form of environmental pollution that upsets people, causes tempers to fray and builds up tension between neighbours. People tolerate a great deal of unnecessary noise even though it often drives them to distraction. Local authority noise patrols can obtain warrants to enter premises where noise and alarms are disturbing the neighbourhood. They can oppose the renewal of licences for noisy pubs. They can apply to the courts for fines of up to R10 000 for persistent noise offenders.

3. Violent crimes, such as rape and murder, are currently rife in South Africa. These crimes warrant the harshest form of punishment, namely, capital punishment. Moreover, violent criminals have renounced their right to protection from the state. Capital punishment affirms the authority of the state to protect its citizens from violent criminals.

Answers

I will supply you with answers to exercises (1) and (3). Apply the knowledge and skills you have gained from the previous exercises and complete exercise (2) on your own.

1. A law that bans the use of marijuana is a bad idea, because anything that would put ordinary social marijuana smokers in jail is a bad idea.

In this argument a *premise is missing*. What is missing is the assumption that links the stated premise to the conclusion: 'A law that bans the use of marijuana would put ordinary social marijuana smokers in jail'. The missing premise in this argument is thus that a law that bans the use of marijuana would put ordinary social marijuana smokers in jail. The structure of this argument can be illustrated as follows:

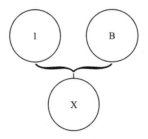

The diagram shows that there is a *missing premise* B. Above we have filled in the missing premise, namely, 'A law that bans the use of marijuana would put ordinary social marijuana smokers in jail'. Premise B is necessary to give sufficient support for the conclusion X. Note that premises 1 and B support the conclusion X interdependently.

3. Violent crimes, such as rape and murder, are currently rife in South Africa. These crimes warrant the harshest form of punishment, namely capital punishment. Moreover, violent criminals have renounced their right to protection from the state. Capital punishment affirms the authority of the state to protect its citizens from violent criminals.

In this argument the premises are supplied, but the *conclusion is missing.* We thus have to fill in the implied conclusion. If you read this passage carefully, understand what the author is trying to say, and think about the meaning of the premises in this argument, then it will be clear to you that the arguer is trying to claim that: Because violent crimes, such as rape and murder, are currently rife in South Africa; and because these crimes warrant the harshest form of punishment, namely capital punishment; and because violent criminals have renounced their right to protection from the state; and because capital punishment affirms the authority of the state to protect its citizens from violent criminals, *capital punishment should be reinstated to stop violent crimes.* The *implicit conclusion* here is: 'Capital punishment should be reinstated to stop violent crimes'. The structure of this argument can be illustrated as follows:

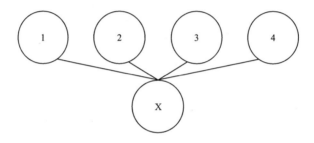

The diagram shows that there is a *missing conclusion,* namely X. From the context of the argument we have drawn our own conclusion, namely, 'Capital punishment should be reinstated to stop violent crimes'. Note that premises 1, 2, 3 and 4 support the conclusion independently.

4   Analysing complex arguments

In the preceding sections we have dealt primarily with shorter passages, which presented simple arguments. In these cases the task of identifying the premises and the conclusion is fairly easy. However, not all arguments are simple and uncomplicated. Some arguments are complex and contain sub-arguments. In such cases, the task of identifying premises and conclusions is more difficult and we have to rely more on our ability to interpret the text. In a longer argument, the conclusion of a sub-argument may serve as a premise for a further sub-argument and, perhaps, the conclusion of this argument will serve as the premise for yet another argument. This kind of complex argument is called a *chain* argument. Consider the following argument, for example:

Unlike most other countries, South Africa does not have adequate public transport. Without adequate public transport, such as fast underground metro trains, our economy and our tourism industry will suffer badly. Therefore, we should do whatever we can to increase our economic growth and promote tourism. It follows from this that the objections to the railway construction of the new Gautrain are short-sighted. Firstly, more people will benefit from the new superfast train than will suffer because of losing their homes and ground. Secondly, those who do lose their homes and ground will be compensated. Thirdly, many jobs will be created by the new railway construction. Fourthly, it will boost our economic growth. And finally, it will promote our tourism industry, especially in view of the 2010 FIFA World Cup.

Let us bracket and number the statements of the above argument:

[Unlike most other countries, South Africa does not have adequate public transport]¹. [Without adequate public transport, such as fast underground metro trains, our economy and our tourism industry will suffer badly]². *Therefore*, [we should do whatever we can to increase our economic growth and promote tourism]³. *It follows from this that* [the objections to the railway construction for the new Gautrain are short-sighted]⁴. *Firstly*, [more people will benefit from the new superfast train than will suffer as a result of losing their homes and ground]⁵. *Secondly*, [those who do lose their homes and ground will be compensated]⁶. *Thirdly*, [many jobs will be created by the new railway construction]⁷. *Fourthly*, [it will boost our economic growth]⁸. And *finally*, [it will promote our tourism industry, especially in view of the 2010 FIFA World Cup]⁹.

We can summarise the structure of the argument as follows:

> **Chain argument**
>
> Main conclusion – 3
> Premises for main conclusion – 1 and 2
> Sub-conclusion – 4
> Premises for sub-conclusion – 3, 5, 6, 7, 8, 9

This is a chain argument, where *two* arguments are presented. The conclusion of the first argument, namely: 'We should do whatever we can to increase our economic growth and promote tourism', serves as a premise for the second argument, which has as its conclusion the following point: 'The objections to the railway construction for the new Gautrain are short-sighted'. The acceptability of the second argument in this complex argument depends, in part, on the acceptability of the first argument.

When you are dealing with a complex argument or an unclear passage, remember that you should consider the argument in the *context* in which it is presented. Ask yourself whether the argument is part of an article whose main point is communicated in the *title*. If this is the case, then ask yourself how the argument is related to the point.

For example, if the title is 'Depression and suicide', look for some point about the relation between depression and suicide. Or perhaps the argument is part of a debate in which the participants have clearly stated which side they support. If so, then the argument or passage may offer premises in support of one of the positions.

It is also helpful, after considering the context, to *simplify and paraphrase* the passage. When you have removed or modified confusing and inessential elements, it will be easier to understand the structure of what is being said. Take care to modify or simplify the author's words in such a way that you do not distort the meaning of what has been said. Your simplification or modification should accurately reflect what is meant in the original text.

5   Steps in analysing arguments

In the next section I summarise the process of analysing simple and complex arguments, which we have been using throughout this chapter, as *steps* that you can follow when you analyse arguments on your own.

5.1   Clarify whether an argument is presented

Read the entire passage and decide if it is an argument. In chapter 3 I explained that an argument is a group of statements. One of these statements is the conclusion of the argument. The other statements are premises that are intended to support the conclusion. I also explained that not every collection of statements makes up an argument. If you have forgotten the information on 'What is an argument?', turn back to chapter 3: 'Working with arguments' and read the section again.

5.2   Bracket and number the statements

Put the statements in brackets and number them in the order in which they appear. Note that a statement asserts or makes a claim about an issue, an idea, or some state of affairs in the world. This means that we cannot just randomly bracket sentences. Make sure that the statements you put in brackets make sense. Bracketing and numbering statements helps us to identify conclusions and premises in arguments.

5.3   Identify the conclusion(s)

Identify the conclusion, or the conclusions if the argument is a chain argument, by underlining the conclusion indicators. If the conclusion is implied, then state the conclusion in full.

5.4 *Identify the premises*

Identify the premises by underlining the premise indicators. Look for premises that lead directly to the conclusion. Decide whether the premises support the conclusion independently or interdependently. Note that there may be both types of premise (those that offer independent support and those that offer interdependent support) in an argument. Fill in the missing premises, if necessary. Here is a useful tactic to remember: when you encounter a passage that contains a lot of non-argumentative prose, pick out the conclusion first; find the statement (or statements) that seems to support the conclusion most directly, and then add the missing or implicit premise(s).

5.5 *Represent the structure of the argument*

A full analysis of the structure of an argument requires identifying the key components of the argument. This means stating what kind of argument it is (a simple or chain argument); identifying the conclusion of the argument; and identifying the premises of the argument. A useful format for presenting the structure of an argument is the following:

> **Chain argument**
>
> Main conclusion – 3
> Premises for main conclusion – 1, 2
> Sub-conclusion – 4
> Premises for sub-conclusion – 3, 5, 6, 7, 8, 9

The above format serves as only one example of how the structure of an argument can be illustrated. The data in the format will be different for different arguments, depending on the particular structure of the argument.

Another format for presenting the structure of an argument is to draw a diagram of the premises and conclusion(s), thereby revealing how the premises are related to the conclusion (as we have done in section 3 above).

> **Remember:** you do not need to draw diagrams to present the structure of the argument each time you want to analyse an argument. This would be extremely time-consuming. We only need to draw diagrams of an argument if we need to establish how the premises and the conclusion(s) of the argument are related.

Exercise

Use the knowledge and competencies that you have acquired in all the previous exercises to analyse the following complex arguments:

1. 'Most parents want their children to have successful careers. Since education is essential to success, it is the duty of parents to give children the best possible education. Because it is also in the country's economic interest to have a highly educated population, the government should help parents to provide for their children's education. Therefore all parents should receive financial help towards the cost of their children's education, so the low paid should receive tax credits and those who are better off should receive tax relief.' (Fisher 2001:24)

2. 'Simple common sense tells us that capital punishment is a more powerful deterrent against crime than prison. The more severe the punishment, the greater the risk to the would-be criminal; and the greater the risk, the more reason not to commit the crime. I'm not saying that every would-be killer is rational enough to weigh the pros and cons before deciding whether to kill, but it certainly stands to reason that some are. And as long as that's true, capital punishment serves its purpose – saving innocent lives'. (Olen & Barry 1999:280)

3. 'We both agree that it's better to work than receive welfare. We also agree that illegitimacy is a serious problem among the young and poor. But one of the biggest flaws of welfare is that it makes being a single mother on welfare an acceptable lifestyle. There used to be a stigma attached to having illegitimate children. Pregnant teenagers were sent to homes for unwed mothers and kept out of sight. There was a stigma attached to taking handouts, too. People were expected to earn their own way. That's a large part of what human dignity was about, and what it should still be about. But now those stigmas are gone. We're telling kids that getting pregnant when they're still in school is nothing to be ashamed of, that it's fine to set up house at the taxpayer's expense. Maybe they're not thinking about welfare when they become pregnant, but you can't deny that welfare produces enough role models for them in poor neighbourhoods.' (Olen & Barry 1999:324)

4. Earlier, in chapter 1, I said that Socrates in his quest for wisdom and truth followed the method of critical inquiry through which he uncovered unsubstantiated knowledge claims. This critical attitude was, however, perceived by the state authorities of Athens as a threat to society and Socrates was sentenced to death. The following is an excerpt of one of Socrates' speeches dealing with his death sentence, which Plato, a student of Socrates, documented in *The Apology* in the year 399 BC:

'I suspect that this thing that has happened to me is a blessing, and we are quite mistaken in supposing death to be evil. ... Death is one of two things. Either it is annihilation, and the dead have no consciousness of anything; or, as we are told, it is really a change: a migration of the soul from this place to another. Now if there is no consciousness but only a dreamless sleep, death must be a marvellous gain. I suppose that if anyone were told to pick out the night on which he slept so soundly as not even to dream, and then to compare it with all the other nights and days of his life, and then were told to say, after due consideration, how many better and happier days and nights than this he had spent in the course of his life – well, I think that the Great King himself, to say nothing of any private person, would find these days and nights easy to count in comparison with the rest. If death is like this, then I call it gain; because the whole of time, if you look at it in this way, can be regarded as no more than one single night. If on the other hand death is a removal from here to some other place, and if what we are told is true, that all the dead are there, what greater blessing could there be than this, gentlemen?' (Plato 1961:74–75)

5. Arthur Schopenhauer (1788–1860) was a German philosopher who claimed that the physical world is phenomenal and exists only for 'the subject of knowledge'. He argued that, while we cannot prove that the rest of nature is more than mere appearance, namely the appearance of something in itself, to deny this would be a form of solipsism (the idea that only the self exists or can be known), something which belongs only to the madhouse. We have to look at the world sanely, and this means that we must suppose that everything in it is the appearance of what in itself is Will, a drive to survive at the expense of others. The following is an excerpt from Schopenhauer's main philosophical work, *The world as will and representation*:

'Work, worry, toil and trouble are indeed the lot of almost all men their whole life long. And yet if every desire were satisfied as soon as it arose how would men occupy their lives, how would they pass the time? Imagine this race transported to a Utopia where everything grows of its own accord and turkeys fly around ready roasted, where lovers find one another without any delay and keep one another without any difficulty: in such a place some men would die of boredom or hang themselves, some would fight and kill one another, and thus they would create for themselves more suffering than nature inflicts on them as it is.' (Schopenhauer 1969:100)

> **Tip:** Here is some guidance to help you analyse this argument. Schopenhauer claims that, because it is the nature of people to labour and struggle, almost all people experience work, toil and trouble throughout their lives. Therefore, in a Utopia (a state of bliss) people would create for themselves more suffering than nature inflicts on them, that is, they would die of boredom or hang themselves or kill one another.

6. 'When prisoners under sentence of death are given the choice between life in prison and execution, 99 per cent of them choose life imprisonment. This shows that they fear death more than they fear life imprisonment. Since one is most deterred by what one most fears, it is evident that the threat of the death penalty is more likely to deter most potential murderers than is the threat of life imprisonment.' (Fisher 2001:181)

Answers

I will supply answers to exercises (1) and (4). Apply your knowledge and skills of analysing arguments and complete exercises (2), (3), (5) and (6) on your own.

Exercise 1

Most parents want their children to have successful careers. Since education is essential to success, it is the duty of parents to give children the best possible education. Because it is also in the country's economic interest to have a highly educated population, the government should help parents to provide for their children's education. Therefore all parents should receive financial help towards the cost of their children's education, so the low paid should receive tax credits and those who are better off should receive tax relief.

We can bracket and number the statements of the argument as follows:

[Most parents want their children to have successful careers][1]. *Since* [education is essential to success][2], [it is the duty of parents to give children the best possible education][3]. *Because* [it is also in the country's economic interest to have a highly educated population][4], [the government should help parents to provide for their children's education][5]. *Therefore* [all parents should receive financial help towards the cost of their children's education][6], *so* [the low paid should receive tax credits and those who are better off should receive tax relief][7].

The structure of the argument can be summarised as follows:

> **Chain argument:**
>
> Main conclusion – 7
> Premise for main conclusion – 6
> Sub-conclusion – 6
> Premise for sub-conclusion – 5
> Sub-conclusion – 5
> Premises for sub-conclusion – 3, 4
> Sub-conclusion – 3
> Premises for sub-conclusion – 1, 2

Note that this chain argument has four conclusions, one main conclusion and three sub-conclusions. The main conclusion (the point the arguer is trying to convince us of) is statement number 7 [the low paid should receive tax credits and those who are better off should receive tax relief]. The main conclusion is supported by statement number 6 [all parents should receive financial help towards the cost of their children's education], which is also a sub-conclusion in the argument. This sub-conclusion is supported by statement number 5 [the government should help parents to provide for their children's education], which in turn serves as another sub-conclusion in the argument. Statement number 5 (the second sub-conclusion) is supported by two premises, statement number 3 [it is the duty of parents to give children the best possible education] and statement number 4 [it is also in the country's economic interest to have a highly educated population]. The third sub-conclusion in the argument is statement number 3 [it is the duty of parents to give children the best possible education], which is supported by the two premises, statement number 1 [most parents want their children to have successful careers] and statement number 2 [education is essential to success].

In order for us to follow the reasoning presented in the argument, let us write this argument out in full:

Reason 1 [most parents want their children to have successful careers] *and reason 2* [education is essential to success], *so* sub-conclusion [it is the duty of parents to give children the best possible education].

Reason 3 [it is the duty of parents to give children the best possible education] *and reason 4* [it is also in the country's economic interest to have a highly educated population], *so* sub-conclusion [the government should help parents to provide for their children's education].

Reason 5 [the government should help parents to provide for their children's education], *therefore* sub-conclusion [all parents should receive financial help towards the cost of their children's education].

Reason 6 [all parents should receive financial help towards the cost of their children's education], *so* main conclusion [the low paid should receive tax credits and those who are better off should receive tax relief].

Exercise 4

> I suspect that this thing that has happened to me is a blessing, and we are quite mistaken in supposing death to be evil. ... Death is one of two things. Either it is annihilation, and the dead have no consciousness of anything; or, as we are told, it is really a change: a migration of the soul from this place to another. Now if there is no consciousness but only a dreamless sleep, death must be a marvellous gain. I suppose that if anyone were told to pick out the night on which he slept so soundly as not even to dream, and then to compare it with all the other nights and days of his life, and then were told to say, after due consideration, how many better and happier days and nights than this he had spent in the course of his life – well, I think that the Great King himself, to say nothing of any private person, would find these days and nights easy to count in comparison with the rest. If death is like this, then I call it gain; because the whole of time, if you look at it in this way, can be regarded as no more than one single night. If on the other hand death is a removal from here to some other place, and if what we are told is true, that all the dead are there, what greater blessing could there be than this, gentlemen?

This is an example of a complex argument that contains a lot of *non-argumentative prose*. We thus have to *rewrite* this argument, using the principle of *charitable interpretation*, so as to draw out the conclusion or conclusions first and then find the statements that support the conclusions most directly. Let us rewrite this argument, considering the *context* in which the argument is presented.

> [I suspect that the sentence to death is a blessing for me][1], and [we are quite mistaken in supposing that death is evil][2]. ... [Death is one of two things][3]. [Either death is annihilation, and the dead have no consciousness of anything][4]; or [death is really a change: a migration of the soul from this place to another][5]. If [there is no consciousness but only a dreamless sleep][6], *then* [death must be a marvellous gain][7]. *If* on the other hand [death is a removal from here to some other place][8], *then* [there is no greater blessing than death][9].

In this argument there are four conclusions. What is the main conclusion of the argument? Here we have to ask ourselves what main point is communicated in the passage. From the context of the argument, it should be clear that Socrates is dealing with his sentence of death. The main point (or conclusion) is that the *death sentence* is a blessing for him (Socrates). The first sub-conclusion is: 'we are mistaken in supposing that death is evil'. In support of this claim, Socrates offers the following reasons: Death is one of two things: either death is annihilation, and the dead have no consciousness of anything, or death is really a change, a migration of the soul from this place to another. The latter claim Socrates seeks to substantiate by offering reasons. He says: *If* there is no consciousness but only a dreamless sleep, *then* death must be a marvellous gain. And *if* death is a removal from here to some other place, *then* there is no greater blessing than death.

We can summarise the structure of the argument as follows:

Chain argument:

Main conclusion – 1
Premises for main conclusion – 2, 3, 4, 5, 6, 7, 8, 9
Sub-conclusion – 2
Premises for sub-conclusion – 3, 4, 5
Sub-conclusion – 7
Premise for sub-conclusion – 6
Sub-conclusion – 9
Premise for sub-conclusion – 8

In summary

As we said right at the beginning, the aim of this chapter is to help you to develop and sharpen your critical reasoning skills in analysing arguments. But why is this important? The analysis of arguments is important because most arguments we come across require us first to analyse their structure *before* we can evaluate them. We cannot evaluate arguments unless we have a grasp of how to analyse arguments: we need to decide which statements are not supported, and which act as premises for a sub-argument. We also need to ask ourselves which statement is the conclusion (what the arguer is trying to persuade us of)? What type of argument is it? Which arguments are valid, strong or weak? Analysing arguments may seem difficult and time-consuming, but the result is a deeper understanding of the meaning of the argument, which serves as a clear and unconfused entry point to evaluating arguments. The evaluation of arguments will be our theme in chapter 6.

Before we can evaluate arguments successfully, we need to understand the role and types of definitions used in arguments. How can we evaluate arguments if we do not know the meaning of the concepts being used in the argument? This is the focus of our next chapter, which deals with the role and types of definitions used in argumentation.

Definitions, counterexamples and counterarguments

It was in vain that Watt said, Pot, pot. Well, perhaps not quite in vain, but very nearly. For it was not a pot, the more he looked, the more he reflected, the more he felt sure of that, that it was not a pot at all. It resembled a pot, it was almost a pot, but it was not a pot of which one could say, Pot, pot, and be comforted. It was in vain that it answered, with unexceptionable adequacy, all the purposes, and performed all the offices, of a pot, it was not a pot.

Samuel Beckett

I n this chapter we will discuss the role and types of definitions used in arguments and the role of counterexamples and counterarguments when evaluating arguments. In chapter 2 ('Obstacles to clear thinking: preconceived ideas and fallacies') we saw that the use of vague and ambiguous terms can obscure our ideas and lead to faulty reasoning. As critical thinkers, we should use words carefully and make sure that the concepts we use in argumentation are properly defined.

1 The role of definitions

Defining the key terms and concepts we use in argumentation helps to reduce vagueness, avoid ambiguities and clarify information. It also prevents misunderstandings.

Michael Andolina (2002:42–43) has the following to say about the importance of definitions in order to clarify information and alleviate potential conflict:

Defining your terms, especially in the beginning of a discussion, establishes the intended meaning and sets boundaries for what you are attempting to communicate. ... [Words and concepts] are the main vehicles through which we communicate our thoughts, feelings, and experiences. However, a mere string of words is inadequate for communicating these experiences in an intelligible way. We need to organize experience under general ideas so that the listener or reader can fully understand what we are trying to convey. Concepts perform that function. Concepts are general ideas that bring order and intelligibility to our experience.

The point Andolina makes is that definitions play an important role in argumentation and communication. The role of definitions is not only to clarify the meaning of words, but also to explain and develop the key concepts we use to communicate our thoughts, feelings and experiences. It is important to define or explain the meaning of the concepts used in arguments, because often the validity or soundness of an argument depends on how the concepts used in it are explained.

Definitions play an important role, not only when we evaluate the arguments of other people, but also when we construct our own arguments. In chapter 8 we will discuss, in detail, the construction of arguments and how to write critical essays – we will therefore return, in chapter 8, to the importance of explaining the meaning of the concepts used in an argument.

An important first step in evaluating arguments is thus to check whether the arguer offers an explanation of the key concepts he or she is using in the argument. Before we can evaluate a definition properly, however, we have to know what kind of definition it is. In the next section we discuss four major types of definitions used in argumentation: denotative definitions, logical definitions, stipulative definitions and persuasive definitions.

2   Types of definitions

2.1 Denotative definitions

Denotative definitions are also called 'definitions by example'. Sometimes, when we are asked to define a word, we are not in a position to provide words that are equivalent, in meaning, to the word we have been asked to define. In these cases it is easier to give a denotation. The word denotation comes from the Latin word *denotare*, which means to mark down. If, for example, we are asked to define the term 'leader', we could say that a leader is 'a man or a woman who shows the way by going first, who effectively leads silently and wisely through deeds and courage'. This definition of a leader is, however, still vague and we might not be able to give all the characteristics a person must have to qualify as a leader. In order to clarify the meaning of the term 'leader', then, it might be a good idea to give examples of leaders.

By giving a denotative definition of the term 'leader' we mark down or give examples of people belonging to the class of leaders. So we can define the term 'leader' by pointing to examples of leaders, such as Abraham Lincoln, Martin

Luther King or Nelson Mandela. Some abstract concepts are difficult to define and arguers may provide us with different and conflicting definitions. This is where denotative definitions are useful. Agreement on the denotation of a term gives us a basis for further discussion. Remember that, when you use denotative definitions, it is best to give as many examples as possible.

2.2 Logical definitions

A logical definition defines a term by selecting those properties that are shared by and confined to all the things that the term covers. When we use logical definitions we should make sure we select those properties that are the distinguishing characteristics of the thing defined. In other words, those characteristics that it alone possesses and that are not possessed by other things. For example, a logical definition of 'mammal' is 'any member of a large class of warm-blooded vertebrates that suckle their young'. A creature with these unique properties is covered by the definition of 'mammal'.

Here is another example of a logical definition: a triangle is a flat shape with three straight sides and three angles. In the case of logical definitions the intention is to give exact explanations of the meanings of concepts, as is often the case in science, mathematics and formal logic. The reason for this is that scientific, mathematical and logical explanations *depend* on exact explanations of the meaning of terms and concepts.

Bear in mind that it would be inappropriate to insist on precise definitions of words we use in everyday language. In ordinary language we use words more loosely and we explain their meaning by giving examples, by drawing contrasts and by stipulating a meaning. In everyday life we use ordinary language more loosely than is the case in science, mathematics or formal logic because, in ordinary language, the meaning of concepts often depends on the context in which they are used and on the particular purpose of use. For example, if a friend says to you that 'he would love to spend time with you because he enjoys your company', you would not run to the dictionary or consult an encyclopaedia or a textbook to determine the precise meaning of the words 'love', 'enjoys', and 'company'. Instead, you would interpret your friend's words simply by assuming that he was using these words in the normal way.

2.3 Stipulative definitions

A stipulative definition stipulates or suggests that a given term should be used in a particular way. A stipulative definition is also called a 'coining definition' because it assigns or 'coins' meaning to a new term. Arguers often use stipulative definitions when terms are vague and ambiguous. It is easy to define the term 'mammal', because there is general consensus about the meaning of the term. It is more difficult to reach consensus about the meaning of abstract terms, such as 'person', 'good', 'justice', 'equality' and 'experience'. People differ about the meanings of these concepts and often have conflicting definitions.

In these cases an arguer may stipulate what he (or she) means by a term for the purpose of his argument. For example, in an argument about abortion an arguer may stipulate that he takes the word 'person' to mean a cluster of features encompassing biological, psychological, rational, social and legal factors. His stipulative definition of 'person' may be the following: 'By "person" I mean a creature who has a certain genetic makeup; who has a concept of self; has the ability to use and understand language; possesses the ability to reason and draw conclusions; can work with others; is subject to the law and is protected by it.'

The arguer could then claim that a fetus is not a person in the sense stipulated by his definition and thus that abortion is morally justified. In this case the acceptability of the argument depends on whether we accept the crucial stipulative definition of 'person' used in the argument.

2.4 Persuasive definitions

A persuasive definition aims at influencing the reader's attitude by suggesting a new meaning for a term that is already in common use. Many words in controversial subjects, such as politics, religion, ethics, and the arts, are subjected to persuasive definitions. Let us take the following example: 'Political power, properly so called, is merely the organized power of one class for oppressing another' (Marx & Engels 1998:61). In this argument Marx and Engels are trying to influence their readers' attitudes and behaviour by creating negative feelings about political power in general, while their criticism is, in fact, aimed at a particular form of political power, namely, capitalism. They are trying to persuade their audience by assigning a different cognitive meaning to the words 'political power' while preserving the emotive force of the words.

We should be suspicious of persuasive definitions because a persuasive definition is a claim camouflaged as a definition. For instance, in an argument about abortion an author defines abortion as the 'murder of unborn children'. This is a persuasive definition because what should be debated, namely the issue of abortion, is being assumed in the definition. We should be aware of persuasive definitions when we evaluate arguments because, sometimes, arguers may use terms in a context of 'reasoning' that is misleading as far as its meaning is concerned and this can mislead us, or persuade us into accepting positions we do not believe in. Likewise, we should avoid using persuasive definitions when we construct our own arguments.

Exercise

Identify the type of definition used in each of the following passages:

1. She is a real madam.
2. *'True culture* is not acquaintance with the arts but with science and technology.' (Example taken from Hospers 1970:54).
3. A chronometer is any instrument designed for measuring time precisely.
4. 'By being "educated" I mean having such an apprehension of the contours of the map of what has been written in the past, as to see instinctively where everything belongs, and approximately where anything new is likely to belong; it means, furthermore, being able to allow for all the books one has not read and the things one does not understand – it means some understanding of one's own ignorance.' (TS Eliot)
5. A feminist is someone who thinks that women are better than men.
6. Hexadecimal numbers are numbers that are based on the number 16 and are mainly used in computers.
7. A good teacher is someone who takes his or her job of teaching to heart, who enables learners to determine what they need to learn through critical questioning and goal-setting and who encourages learners to revisit problems from different perspectives and to arrive at their own conclusions.
8. By 'argument' I mean a group of statements that intend to affirm the truth or validity of a claim.

Answers

1. Persuasive definition
2. Persuasive definition
3. Logical definition
4. Stipulative definition
5. Persuasive definition
6. Logical definition
7. Denotative definition
8. Stipulative definition

3   The role of counterexamples and counterarguments

Counterexamples and counterarguments play an important role in argumentation. When we evaluate the premises and conclusions of an argument it is important to be aware of possible counterexamples. A useful way to evaluate claims made in an argument is to construct counterexamples to those claims. Constructing counterexamples is an effective way of testing the validity of an argument's claims. A valid counterexample can defeat a claim. Let us look at the following example:

All women are bad drivers.

It takes one example of a good woman driver to counter and defeat this claim.

Let us look at another example:

Any act of killing a person is murder. Thus killing a fetus is murder.

Besides the fact that this is a bad argument, as it is debatable whether a fetus is a person and the arguer does not define what he or she means by the concept of a 'person', the argument can easily be refuted by a counterexample. We can challenge this argument by constructing the following counterexample: self-defence may result in the killing of a person, but the act of self-defence does not usually count as murder.

There is a difference between a counterexample and a counterargument. The difference lies in the following: a *counterexample* differs from a counterargument in that a counterexample is a specific example which defeats or runs counter to the claim made in an argument. Note that generalisations are most open to refutation by counterexamples. In the example above, the general claim 'All women are bad drivers' is easily defeated by one example of an excellent woman driver. The argument ends right there and there is nothing more to be said. Note that *particular* statements or examples are required to refute generalisations.

A *counterargument* is an argument an arguer constructs in answer to another argument. Such an argument may not be the last word. An opponent might well reply to the counterargument, whereupon the arguer may construct another counterargument, and so on.

Counterexamples and counterarguments play an important role in evaluating and constructing arguments. A good way of testing the plausibility or the truth of claims made in an argument is to attempt to construct counterexamples or counterarguments to the claims made by the arguer. Counterexamples and counterarguments challenge arguments by flushing out assumptions, preconceived ideas, fallacies and generalisations.

Exercise

1. Construct counterexamples to the following claims:

   (a) Men make poor parents because men are not inclined toward nurturing and caring for children.

   (b) It is always wrong to break a promise.

   (c) A morally good action is one based on the principle of utility, that is, the greatest happiness for the greatest number of people.

   (d) Democracy is the best form of government because it is based on the principle of negotiation and inclusion.

2. Construct a counterargument to the following argument:

   (a) Statistics have shown that soap advertising does not lead to increased use of soap, but instead to switching brands of soap. Likewise, the advertising of tobacco does not lead to increased use of tobacco, but to switching cigarette brands. Therefore, the banning of tobacco advertising does not discourage the use of tobacco by those who smoke. (Adapted from Fletcher 1978: 227)

   (b) Since fetuses are nothing more than bundles of living tissue, bombarding fetuses that are about to be aborted with ultrasound and then doing autopsies on them after abortion are justifiable actions. Thus, there is nothing wrong with our scientific organisation's decision to use fetuses to conduct research into the effects of ultrasound on human beings.

Answers

I will help you with answers to exercises 1 (a), 1 (b) and 2 (a). Apply the knowledge and competencies you have gained from the previous exercises and do the rest of the exercises on your own.

1 (a) To defeat the claim 'Men make poor parents because men are not inclined toward nurturing and caring for children', one only needs to construct one counterexample of a case where a man nurtured and cared successfully for his children. This counterexample would defeat the claim that men make poor parents.

   (b) One possible counterexample to the claim 'It is always wrong to break a promise', is: breaking a promise in a war situation could well be morally justifiable if doing so saved the lives of thousands of innocent people.

2   (a)   Statistics have shown that soap advertising does not lead to increased use of soap, but instead to switching brands of soap. Likewise, the advertising of tobacco does not lead to increased use of tobacco, but to switching cigarette brands. Therefore, the banning of tobacco advertising does not discourage the use of tobacco by people who smoke.

Two counterarguments could be constructed against the point made in the argument above:

(i)   The comparison between the use of soap and the use of tobacco does not hold. The use of soap is a necessity among people in most countries for hygiene purposes, while the use of tobacco is not a necessity, but optional and a matter of choice.

(ii)   The banning of tobacco advertising *may well have* the effect of discouraging the use of tobacco among the public at large, especially among members of the public who are thinking about taking up smoking or who smoke already.

In summary

In this chapter we have explained the role and types of definitions used in arguments. The point is not to memorise these definitions, but to understand the role that definitions play in argumentation. We should develop a knack for clarifying the meaning of key concepts that are used in arguments. This will help us to avoid the use of vague and ambiguous terms that can obscure our ideas and lead to faulty reasoning. Likewise, when we evaluate arguments, we should be on the lookout for ill-defined and ambiguous concepts used in argumentation because, very often, the validity of an argument depends on how the arguer defines the key concepts used in his or her argument.

In this chapter we have also discussed the role of counterexamples and counterarguments in arguments. We have seen that a useful way of testing the validity of an argument's claims is to construct counterexamples and counterarguments. Try to apply the knowledge and competencies you have acquired in this chapter to the evaluation of arguments, which is the focus of the next chapter.

Evaluating arguments

Read not to contradict and confute, nor to believe and take for granted ... but to weigh and consider.

Francis Bacon

In chapters 3 and 4 we discussed the analysis of arguments. Analysing arguments is, however, only one aspect of critical reasoning. Another important aspect of critical reasoning is *evaluating* arguments, that is, being able to judge, accurately, whether arguments are valid and sound. Simply put, when we evaluate an argument we decide whether we should be persuaded by it.

Evaluating an argument entails more than just criticising the argument. It involves critically examining the plausibility of the claims that have been made; critically considering assumptions, preconceived ideas and faulty reasoning; weighing possible solutions; clarifying issues; making informed and reasoned decisions; forming one's own opinions on issues and locating issues within a global perspective.

In the previous chapter you learnt how to use techniques for analysing arguments and we pointed out that analysing an argument is the 'entry point' to evaluating an argument. This chapter contains specialised information that is crucial in understanding and evaluating arguments. We will explore the following issues: the difference between empirical arguments and value arguments; the difference between deductive and inductive arguments; the difference between validity and soundness; three types of inductive reasoning; and the criteria for distinguishing good arguments from bad ones. You need to be able to do all this in order to evaluate arguments accurately. We will deal with each issue systematically.

1   Understanding arguments

The evaluation of arguments requires an *understanding* of the type of argument being evaluated. This is because, before we can critically examine the soundness of claims, we must know what kind of argument we are dealing with. Keep in mind that different evaluative approaches are required, depending on the type of argument we are dealing with. In this chapter I will explain four types of arguments: empirical, value, deductive and inductive arguments. Before we engage in a discussion of the different types of arguments, I will provide you with a short definition and example of each type of argument:

Empirical argument. An empirical argument is an argument in which the premises assert that some empirically determinable facts apply. The correctness or otherwise of the premises of an empirical argument can be verified or falsified by appealing to factual evidence. The following is an example of an empirical argument:

> I arrived at work at 08:00 this morning.
> The clock system on my computer at work states that I clocked in at 08:00 this morning.
> *Thus*, it is a fact that I arrived at work at 08:00 this morning.

Value argument. A value argument asserts a judgement of taste or a moral claim about right and wrong, good and bad. The truth or correctness of the premises of a value argument depends on argumentation and on substantiated reasons in support of the conclusion of the argument. An example of a value argument is:

> The killing of human beings can never be morally justified.
> Euthanasia is the killing of human beings.
> *Therefore*, euthanasia can never be morally justified.

Deductive argument. A deductive argument is an argument in which the premises are *claimed* to give sufficient support for the conclusion to follow. The following is an example of a deductive argument:

> No animal lover would mistreat a pet.
> Beth is an animal lover.
> *Therefore*, Beth will not mistreat a pet.

Inductive argument. An inductive argument is an argument in which the conclusion is subject to *probability,* even if the premises are assumed to be true. Here is an example of an inductive argument:

> Most first-year students who come from poor educational backgrounds fail their first year at university.
> Peter is a first-year student who comes from a poor educational background.
> *Therefore*, probably, he will fail his first year at university.

Let us now discuss each kind of argument in more detail.

2   Empirical arguments

Empirical arguments are about *facts.* The premises are supposed to provide sufficient empirical evidence to support the conclusion, or convince the audience that the conclusion is true. Consider the following argument:

> There are probably crested barbets in my garden.
> I just heard a crested barbet singing in my garden.
> *Therefore*, there are crested barbets in my garden.

This is an empirical argument because the truth of the premises, 'There are problably crested barbets in my garden' and 'I just heard a crested barbet singing in my garden' can be empirically verified. In other words, we can prove that the premises are true (or false) by using our senses. The premises can be verified by direct observation.

Let us look at another example:

> Healthy lungs are crucial for your health and wellbeing.
> Smoking damages your lungs.
> *Therefore*, smoking is bad for you.

The premises in this argument can be verified empirically because they present observable evidence that the conclusion is true. Empirical arguments are about *facts* and the truth or correctness of the premises of an empirical argument does not depend on what I believe or value.

3   Value arguments

In this section we deal with an important aspect of critical reasoning, namely, *value arguments*. In your study of this text and in other fields of study, such as psychology, sociology, political science, historical studies and so on, you have probably come across arguments about values. Values are important in our lives, because our values determine the decisions we make. Our values determine the judgements we make about other people and *they* inform our judgements about art, literature, music, socio-political issues and so on. Finally, our values determine our decisions about morality and moral truth.

Value arguments are about *values* and not about facts. For example, it is a *fact* that sugar sweetens coffee, but it is a *value* statement that coffee with sugar tastes better than unsweetened coffee. When you say that coffee with sugar tastes better than unsweetened coffee, you are making a value statement. This kind of value statement is based on your subjective taste and preference, so it would be pointless for anyone to argue with you about your personal taste and preference. Values expressing personal preferences are not controversial and they are usually not problematic.

There are, however, other kinds of values that are controversial and therefore problematic, namely *moral values*. They are problematic because they cannot be verified or falsified by appealing to evidence (or lack of evidence) or the senses (which we can do in the case of empirical statements).

In addition, we cannot assume that most people hold the same values. In other words, it is difficult to determine whether moral value statements are true or false, right or wrong. For example, imagine that you are faced with a moral dilemma: your grandmother is 75 years old and she has been in a coma for 10 years after suffering a stroke. You, in consultation with your family members, have to decide whether or not to switch off the machines that are keeping your grandmother alive. (Switching off the machines would be an act of euthanasia — a term you have come across earlier on in this text.) What would you do? Keep in mind that we can distinguish between four types of euthanasia: *Active voluntary euthanasia* occurs when a competent adult patient requests or gives explicit consent (that is, the person understands what he or she is agreeing to) to certain medical treatment or non-treatment. In some cases of active voluntary euthanasia, the patient requests to be given a lethal injection. *Active involuntary euthanasia* occurs where a patient is competent to make decisions, does not consent or request euthanasia, but a third person, out of pity or for whatever reason, decides to perform euthanasia on the patient by, for instance, administering a fatal drug overdose. This kind of conduct is unlawful and amounts to murder. No legal system tolerates such conduct. *Passive voluntary euthanasia* occurs when a patient chooses to die by refusing treatment, or instructs others to act on his or her behalf. For instance, a terminally ill patient can appoint his or her spouse, family or a lawyer as proxy decision-maker to cease life-sustaining treatment in the event that he or she is incapable of doing so. *Passive involuntary euthanasia* refers to cases of euthanasia where the decision about death is not made by the person whose life is at issue, but by others. These cases include situations where patients are incompetent to give informed consent to life-or-death decisions and others, usually the family, have to make important decisions for them.

The moral dilemma that you and your family are confronted with amounts to deciding whether or not to switch off the machines that are keeping your grandmother alive. Keeping your grandmother alive artificially by machines is also costing your family a great deal of money. Switching off the machines would be an act of *passive involuntary euthanasia*. This is a very difficult decision because you and your family have to determine what your grandmother, who is incompetent to make a decide herself, would have wanted. The decision is whether or not it is better for your grandmother to be dead rather than alive, that is, being kept alive by machines. In this case it is extremely difficult to determine whether your moral decision is right or wrong. The choice that you and your family make would be informed by your moral values.

Value claims differ from claims about facts because, in the case of value claims, there are no objective grounds for correctness. The way we evaluate and justify value statements also differs from the way we justify empirical statements.

When I say, for example, that the door of my office is closed, my claim is either correct or incorrect. It is an empirical claim and what makes it correct is some independent state of affairs in the world. The correctness of my claim does not depend on what I feel or prefer, or even believe. However, when I claim that passive involuntary euthanasia (that is, terminating the life of a patient, who has not indicated his or her wish to die, by ceasing life-support treatment) is morally acceptable, there are no independent facts against which to judge the correctness or incorrectness of my claim.

Some philosophers argue that the same reasoning applies to claims concerning right and wrong, good and bad, justice and injustice. They say that, when I claim that acts of euthanasia are morally correct, I am merely expressing a personal preference. Many philosophers have, however, challenged the view that value claims are merely subjective and they argue that we can, in fact, arrive at objective value statements. The philosophical arguments about whether value claims are subjective or objective are complicated and we will not enter into this dispute here.

What we are concerned about, though, is the question: is there any point in arguing about value claims if they are really only expressions of subjective preference? The answer to this question is that there is some point in arguing about value claims if we can say, firstly, that an arguer can use reason in an argument to persuade us about what is good or bad, right or wrong. This entails critically evaluating our own or other people's views of what is good and bad, right and wrong, just and unjust. The fact that we live in organised communities, cities and countries requires that we develop and rely on widely shared, reason-based views relating to justice, fairness and moral ideals.

Secondly, there is a point to arguing about claims concerning values if there is some way of telling good from bad value arguments. I will show you that ethical arguments expressing value claims can be stated badly or well. As you will see later on in this chapter, a good argument is a sound argument. An argument is sound if the conclusion follows from the premises *and* if the premises or reasons given for the conclusion are acceptable. On the other hand, an argument is poor when it is fallacious or when the reasons advanced are neither true nor certain.

Exercise

What kind of statements are the following?
1. I prefer Johnny Clegg and Savuka to Bach.
2. Active voluntary euthanasia is ethically justified, while active involuntary euthanasia amounts to murder.
3. This painting is valuable.
4. My car is out of petrol.
5. The death penalty is cruel, unworthy of a civilised society, and morally wrong.
6. A fetus does not have the capacity to make rational decisions.

Answers

1. A value statement.
2. A value statement.
3. An empirical statement, if one takes 'valuable' to mean expensive.
4. An empirical statement.
5. A value statement.
6. A value statement.

In summary, *argumentation* is not straightforward. It is difficult, for instance, to evaluate value arguments because they always involve some *value assumptions*. For example, if someone claims that lying is *always* wrong, and that saving a life is *always* right, you will have difficulties establishing the truth of these value statements. There are, however, ways of telling *good from bad value arguments*. These ways will be discussed at the end of this chapter.

4   Deductive arguments

Deductive reasoning is reasoning which evaluates or constructs deductive arguments. An argument is said to be deductive when the premises are supposed to give sufficient support for the conclusion to follow. Deductive reasoning arrives at a specific conclusion based on generalisations. Differently put, in deductive reasoning general principles or conditions, which we know to be true, or we assume to be true for the circumstances, are applied to specific cases or situations.

Consider the following example of a deductive argument and hence of deductive reasoning:

All human beings are mortal.
Nelson Mandela is a human being.
Therefore, Nelson Mandela is mortal.

Here is another example of a deductive argument:

All killing of human beings is morally wrong.
Abortion is the killing (the termination of a fetus) of a human being.
Therefore, abortion is morally wrong.

Earlier on, we defined a deductive argument as an argument in which the premises are intended to give sufficient support for the conclusion to follow. If the premises give sufficient support for the conclusion to follow then the argument is deductively valid. But does this mean that the argument is sound? That depends on various things. *Not all valid deductive arguments are sound. There is a difference between the validity and the soundness of arguments*, as you will see later.

For now, let us first explore two types of deductive arguments: valid deductive arguments, and invalid deductive arguments.

4.1 *Valid deductive arguments*

A *valid* deductive argument is one in which the structure is valid *and* where the premises offer sufficient support for the conclusion. The following is an example of a valid deductive argument:

If the moon is full, it is circular.
The moon is full.
Therefore, the moon is circular.

Let us first examine the *structure* of this argument and then explore whether the premises of this deductive argument offer sufficient support for the conclusion.

The structure of this argument can be presented as follows:

[If the moon is full, then it is circular][1].
[The moon is full][2].
Therefore [the moon is circular][3].

Conclusion: 3
Premises: 1, 2

The structure of this argument is valid and can be presented as follows:

1. If P, then Q   [If the moon is full, then it is circular]
2. P [The moon is full]
    $\therefore Q$ [Therefore, the moon is circular]

The validity of a deductive argument does not depend, however, only on whether its structure is valid or not. The validity of deductive arguments also depends on whether the premises provide *sufficient support* for the conclusion. To test whether the premises provide sufficient support for the conclusion of a deductive argument, we need to establish whether the conclusion follows *logically* from the premises. Let us return to our example and determine whether the premises of this deductive argument offer sufficient support for its conclusion.

[If the moon is full, then it is circular][1].
[The moon is full][2].
Therefore [the moon is circular][3].

Conclusion – 3
Premises – 1, 2

The premises of the argument offer sufficient support for the conclusion. Premise 1 states 'If the moon is full, then it is circular' and premise 2 states 'The moon is full'. The only logical conclusion we can draw from these two premises is 'The moon is circular'. Given the sufficient support of the premises in this deductive argument, we cannot draw any other conclusion, except that the moon is circular (round). If we encounter a deductive argument with a valid structure and premises that give sufficient support for the conclusion, then we are logically compelled to accept the conclusion of the argument.

Exercise

Consider the following deductive argument and then answer the questions that follow:

All unmarried men are bachelors.
Bongani is an unmarried man.
Therefore, Bongani is a bachelor.

1. How would you present the structure of the above argument?
2. Is the structure of this argument valid?
3. Do the premises of the argument provide adequate support for the conclusion?

Answers

1. The structure of this argument can be presented as follows:

    [All unmarried men are bachelors][1].
    [Bongani is an unmarried man][2].
    Therefore, [Bongani is a bachelor][3].

    Conclusion: 3
    Premises: 1, 2

2. The structure of this argument is valid.

    (1)   All S are P   [Where S = All unmarried men; and P = bachelors]

    (2)   *X is S*   [Where X = Bongani; and S = unmarried man]

    ∴ X is P   [Where X = Bongani; and P = bachelor]

    (1)   All unmarried men are bachelors.

    (2)   Bongani is an unmarried man.

    Therefore, Bongani is a bachelor.

3. The premises of the argument offer sufficient support for the conclusion. If we *assume* the premises to be true, then the conclusion would follow logically. Premise 1 states 'All unmarried men are bachelors' and premise 2 states 'Bongani is an unmarried man'. The only logical conclusion we can draw from these two premises is 'Bongani is a bachelor'. Given the support of the premises in this argument, we cannot draw any other conclusion, except that Bongani is a bachelor.

To summarise, a *valid deductive argument* is an argument with a valid structure *and* premises that offer sufficient support for accepting the conclusion of the argument. The premises of a valid deductive argument logically imply the conclusion and to deny the conclusion would be self-contradictory.

4.2 Invalid deductive arguments

An *invalid* deductive argument is an argument in which the premises fail to give sufficient support for the conclusion. Here is an example of an invalid deductive argument:

If there is a thunderstorm today, my dog will escape through the gate.
My dog escaped through the gate.
Therefore, there was a thunderstorm today.

This argument is invalid because, even if we assume that the two premises are true, it does not necessarily follow that 'there was a thunderstorm today'. The conclusion could be false even if the premises were true. The dog could have escaped through the gate because she was scared of fireworks blasting in the neighbourhood, or because she wanted to protect her territory by chasing the neighbour's annoying cat, which was sitting in a tree just outside the gate.

Note that the structure of the argument is invalid. The structure of the argument can be presented as follows:

> [If there is a thunderstorm today, my dog will escape through the gate][1].
> [My dog escaped through the gate][2].
> *Therefore*, [there was a thunderstorm today][3].

Conclusion: 3
Premises: 1, 2.

(1)   If P, then Q   [If there is a thunderstorm today, then my dog will escape through the gate].

(2) Q [My dog escaped through the gate].

∴ P   [Therefore, there was a thunderstorm today].

This argument is an example of the fallacy of affirming the consequent. Remember that, when we discussed the fallacy of affirming the consequent in chapter 2 ('Obstacles to clear thinking: preconceived ideas and fallacies'), we explained that this fallacy arises because of an invalid structure. The example we used was:

Valid structure	Invalid structure (fallacious)
Modus ponens (Affirming the antecedent)	Affirming the consequent
(1) If P, then Q	(1) If P, then Q
(2) P ∴ Q	(2) Q ∴ P
Example	Example
(1) If my car is out of petrol, then it won't start.	(1) If my car is out of petrol, then it won't start.
(2) My car is out of petrol. (This premise affirms the antecedent.)	(2) My car won't start. (This premise affirms the consequent.)
Therefore: My car won't start.	Therefore: My car is out of petrol.

Note that the structure of the argument on the left-hand side is valid, while the structure of the argument on the right-hand side is invalid. (If you have forgotten this fallacy, turn back to chapter 2 and read through the section on 'Affirming the consequent' again.)

5   Validity versus soundness

In the previous section we examined the difference between valid and invalid deductive arguments. The knowledge and insight you have gained from exploring deductive arguments point to a key issue in critical reasoning and the evaluation of arguments, namely:

> When we evaluate arguments, it is important to keep in mind that *validity is not the same as soundness.*

Remember that a valid deductive argument is an argument with a valid structure and premises that offer sufficient support for the conclusion that follows. This does not imply, though, that the premises *are actually true claims.* Even though the premises of a valid deductive argument give adequate support for the conclusion, those premises could be false. We can say this differently: even if the premises of a deductive argument are entirely false, the argument could still be valid. A valid deductive argument does not have to have true premises, because its *validity* depends on the argument's form or structure, and not on the plausibility or *soundness* of its claims.

Note that arguers sometimes use deductive arguments that are valid, but *not sound*, to persuade their readers to their point of view.

Take, for example, the following argument:

Every act of deliberately killing a human being is wrong.
Euthanasia (the act of mercy killing) is the deliberate killing of a human being.
Therefore, euthanasia is wrong.

Let us analyse the argument to reveal its structure:

[Every act of deliberately killing a human being is wrong][1].
[Euthanasia is the deliberate killing of a human being][2].
Therefore, [euthanasia is wrong][3].

Conclusion: 3
Premises: 1, 2

The structure of this argument is valid and the premises give sufficient support for the conclusion. However, when we evaluate the premises of the argument, we see that the premises are *not plausible or sound*. While it may be true that deliberately killing humans is wrong, it does not follow from this that *euthanasia* is the deliberate *killing* of a human being. It is debatable whether euthanasia (active or passive) is the same as deliberately killing humans. What if a terminally ill patient chooses to die by refusing treatment, or instructs others to act on his or her behalf by appointing the spouse, family or a lawyer as proxy decision-maker to cease life-sustaining treatment in the event that he or she is incapable of doing so? Is this form of euthanasia the *deliberate killing* of a human being? This argument is valid but it is *not sound*, because one of its premises is false and does not give adequate evidence for the conclusion to follow. The conclusion is thus unacceptable.

We can distinguish between validity and soundness as follows:

> *Validity* refers to the relationship between the premises and the conclusion of an argument. It is a structural issue, not an issue of truth or soundness.

> *Soundness* refers to the truth or strength of the premises of an argument. When we assess the soundness of an argument, we want to establish whether or not the evidence provided by the premises is actually true.

Exercise

Consider these two arguments and then answer the questions that follow:

1. All men on the moon have green hair. Socrates is a man on the moon. Therefore, Socrates has green hair.

    (a)   Is the argument valid? Explain your answer.

    (b)   Is the argument sound? Give reasons for your answer.

2. If Barak Obama becomes the President of the United States of America, then he will be the first black President elected in the history of America. Obama became the President of the United States America. Therefore, Obama is the first black President elected in the history of America.

    (a)   Is the argument valid? Explain your answer.

    (b)   Is the argument sound? Give reasons for your answer.

Answers

1. (a) To determine whether the argument is valid, we need to examine its structure. The structure of the argument can be presented as follows:

> [All men on the moon have green hair][1].
> [Socrates is a man on the moon][2].
> *Therefore*, [Socrates has green hair][3].

Conclusion: 3
Premises: 1, 2

The structure of this argument is valid.

(1) All S are P   [All men on the moon have green hair.]

(2) *X is S*   *[Socrates is a man on the moon.]*

∴ X is P   [Therefore, Socrates has green hair.]

The premises of the argument offer sufficient support for the conclusion. In other words, the conclusion follows logically from the premises. Given the sufficient support of the premises in this argument, we cannot draw any other conclusion, except that Socrates has green hair.

The argument is valid because its structure is valid: its premises provide sufficient *support* for the conclusion that follows. However, the content of the argument is obviously absurd and senseless.

(b) The argument is *unsound* because, when we evaluate the premises of the argument, it is clear that the premises are not true. This argument is valid, but it is *unsound*, because the premises do not give adequate *evidence* (based on facts, experience or observation) for the conclusion to be true.

2. (a) The structure of the argument can be presented as follows:

> [If Barak Obama becomes the President of the United States of America, then he will be the first black President elected in the history of America][1].
> [Obama became the President of the United States of America][2].
> *Therefore*, [Obama is the first black President elected in the history of America][3].

Conclusion: 3
Premises: 1, 2

The structure of the argument is valid.

Modus ponens (Affirming the antecedent)

(1) If P, then Q [If Barak Obama becomes the President of the United States of America, then he will be the first Black President elected in the history of America.]

(2) *P*   [Obama became the President of the United States of America.]
∴ Q

Therefore, [Obama is the first Black President elected in the history of America]

The argument is valid because, if we assume the premises to be true, the conclusion could not be false.

(b)   The argument is *sound* because, when we evaluate the premises of the argument, it is clear that the premises are *true* and offer sufficient *evidence* (based on facts, experience or observation) for the conclusion to be true.

In summary, you have learnt: the difference between valid and invalid deductive arguments; the difference between the validity and the soundness of arguments; and that valid deductive arguments are not necessarily sound.

In the next section, we shall discuss inductive arguments. First we explore what inductive reasoning means and then we distinguish between three types of inductive reasoning.

6   Inductive arguments

Inductive reasoning is reasoning that takes us beyond the limits of existing evidence to conclusions about the unknown. The premises of an inductive argument indicate some degree of support for the conclusion, but do not entail the conclusion. The conclusion of an inductive argument is regarded as a hypothesis because the conclusion can only be said to follow *with probability*. When we argue inductively we infer something beyond the contents of the premises (this is referred to as the *inductive 'leap'*). Inductive reasoning moves from specific cases and observations to more general underlying principles or hypotheses that explain them (for example, Einstein's theory of relativity). Inductive reasoning is more open-ended and exploratory than deductive reasoning.

Consider the following example of an inductive argument and hence of inductive reasoning:

Students who get good marks study about three hours a day.
You want good marks.
So, all you have to do to get good marks is study three hours a day.

This argument implies something that the premises do not say. In this argument, the premises do not give *conclusive* evidence that three hours of study a day will result in good marks. Most scientific and mathematical discoveries are made by using inductive reasoning.

Here is another example of an inductive argument:

> Many individual cases of teenagers who abuse drugs came to me for counselling. As a counsellor I have found that most of those teenagers who came to me and confessed to taking drugs have serious family problems.
> *Therefore*, most teenagers who abuse drugs have serious family problems.

The conclusion of this inductive argument can only be said to follow *with probability.* It is important to note that an inductively sound argument, unlike a deductively sound argument, may have a false conclusion. In other words, the truth of the premises of an inductively sound argument makes the truth of the conclusion *probable*, but does not guarantee it. That is why we said that inductive reasoning is more open-ended and exploratory than deductive reasoning. In the next section ('The difference between deductive and inductive arguments') we will look at the difference between deductive and inductive arguments more closely.

For now, let us first explore the difference between three major types of inductive reasoning, namely: statistical extrapolations; arguments from analogy; and arguments using cause-and-effect reasoning.

6.1 *Statistical extrapolations*

This kind of inductive reasoning is quite common. Arguers often strengthen their arguments by referring to some statistical study or evidence. Here is an example of an inductive argument based on statistical data:

> In a recent poll it was established that 600 000 out of one million people in South Africa intended to vote for the ANC. Thus, we can predict that 60 percent of all voters will vote for the ANC in the next election.

Here a poll of the voting intentions of some thousands of voters is used to predict the voting intentions of millions of voters. This sample meets the requirements for good inductive inference: it extrapolates from the statistical data that 60 percent of the voters will vote for the ANC in the next election (and, indeed, based on the evidence, it is likely that they will).

6.2 *Arguments from analogy*

An argument based on analogy compares two cases and points to a common feature or principle in both cases.

The following argument is an example of reasoning by analogy. It is an extract from an article on the problem of abortion written by Judith Jarvis Thomson (1999:189):

> I propose, then, that we grant that the fetus is a person from the moment of conception. How does the argument go from here? Something like this, I take it. Every person has a right to life. So the fetus has a right to life. No doubt the mother has a right to decide what shall happen in and to her body; everyone would grant that. But surely a person's right to life is stronger and more stringent than the mother's right to decide what happens in and to her body, and so outweighs it. So the fetus may not be killed; an abortion may not be performed.
>
> It sounds plausible. But now let me ask you to imagine this. You wake up in the morning and find yourself back to back in bed with an unconscious violinist. A famous unconscious violinist. He has been found to have a fatal kidney ailment, and the Society of Music Lovers has canvassed all available medical records and found that you alone have the right blood type to help. They have therefore kidnapped you, and last night the violinist's circulatory system was plugged into yours, so that your kidneys can be used to extract poisons from his blood as well as your own. The director of the hospital now tells you, 'Look, we're sorry the Society of Music Lovers did this to you — we would never have permitted it if we had known. But still, they did it, and the violinist now is plugged into you. To unplug you would be to kill him. But never mind, it's only for nine months. By then he will have recovered from his ailment, and can safely be unplugged from you.' Is it morally incumbent on you to accede to this situation? No doubt it would be very nice of you if you did a great kindness. But do you have to accede to it? What if it were not nine months, but nine years? Or longer still? What if the director of the hospital says, 'Tough luck, I agree, but you've got to now stay in bed, with the violinist plugged into you for the rest of your life. Because remember this. All persons have a right to life, and violinists are persons. Granted you have a right to decide what happens in and to your body, but a person's right to life outweighs your right to decide what happens in and to your body. So you cannot ever be unplugged from him.' I imagine you would regard this as outrageous, which suggests that something really is wrong with that plausible-sounding argument I mentioned a moment ago.

This is an inductive argument, where the author uses an analogy. She compares a familiar situation (pregnancy) to something unfamiliar (the imaginary situation of having a violinist 'plugged into' you), and then points to a common feature or principle: the responsibility (or is it a burden?) of the 'host' to support another's life. The author uses this kind of inductive reasoning to challenge the reader to question some basic philosophical assumptions about the rights of a fetus and the rights of a mother.

6.3 *Arguments using cause-and-effect reasoning*

When dealing with inductive arguments using cause-and-effect reasoning, take care not to confuse *correlation* with *cause*. Correlation means that two things or events are closely related. Cause means that a certain fact or event produced something else, its effect or result. For example, there may be a correlation between my dog's depression and my working on this manuscript on critical reasoning, but this does not mean that my working on my manuscript caused my dog's depression. Her depression might be caused by a hormonal imbalance.

Causal reasoning is a form of inductive reasoning. If we say that events of type X cause events of type Y, then we are inferring from a limited number of present and past events to an unlimited number of future events. The following is an example of causal reasoning:

Industrial pollutants caused allergic reactions in specific cases of small children in Johannesburg.

Industrial pollutants caused allergic reactions in specific cases of small children in Bloemfontein.

Industrial pollutants caused allergic reactions in specific cases of small children in the Eastern Cape.

Industrial pollutants caused allergic reactions in specific cases of small children in Zimbabwe.

Industrial pollutants caused allergic reactions in specific cases of small children in London.

Industrial pollutants caused allergic reactions in specific cases of small children in New York.

Industrial pollutants caused allergic reactions in specific cases of small children in Detroit.

Thus industrial pollutants cause allergic reactions in all small children.

In the example above, the arguer infers from specific cases of children who are affected by industrial pollutants to the effect of pollutants on *all* small children.

> **Note** that value arguments may be deductive or inductive. The same goes for empirical arguments. Some empirical arguments are deductive, while others are inductive.

The next four examples will illustrate this point:

Example 1

> Every act of deliberately killing a human being is wrong.
> Euthanasia is the deliberate killing of a human being.
> *Therefore*, euthanasia is wrong.

This is an example of a deductive value argument.

Example 2

> A fetus does not have the capacity to think.
> It cannot make rational decisions.
> It cannot be considered a moral agent.
> *Therefore*, abortion is morally justified.

This is an inductive value argument.

Example 3

> If there is a thunderstorm today, my dog will escape through the gate.
> My dog escaped through the gate.
> *Therefore*, there was a thunderstorm today.

This is an example of a deductive empirical argument.

Example 4

> The famous composer Ludwig Beethoven practised for five hours a day.
> You want to be a famous composer.
> *Thus*, all you have to do to be a famous composer is to practise for five hours a day.

This argument is an inductive empirical argument.

7   The difference between deductive and inductive arguments

In order to get a better idea of the meaning of the concepts 'deduction' and 'induction', let us explain the difference between deductive and inductive reasoning.

The difference between a deductive and an inductive argument is that, in a deductive argument, the premises already contain the conclusion, whereas in an inductive argument the conclusion supplies more information than is contained in its premises.

In deductive arguments, the conclusion usually restates information from the premises. Let us take two examples of *deductive reasoning* and note how the conclusion restates information from the premises:

Example 1

If the moon is full, it is circular.
The moon is full.
Therefore, the moon is circular.

Example 2

All men are mortal.
Socrates is a man.
Therefore, Socrates is mortal.

Note that the conclusions of these deductive arguments do not imply something extra and, in fact, repeat the information stated in the premises. The problem with deductive arguments is that their conclusions do not contain new information and thus do not add to our knowledge. In order to make progress, in the scientific world and in everyday life, we need new information. We have to infer things for ourselves by using inductive reasoning (making an inductive 'leap').

Another difference between deductive and inductive arguments is that, in the case of a deductive argument, the premises are claimed to give sufficient support for the conclusion to follow, whereas in an inductive argument the premises provide some support, but never conclusive support, for the conclusion that follows. In an inductive argument, the conclusion can only be said to follow with probability, even if the premises are assumed to be true. If the premises of a deductive argument offer sufficient support for the conclusion, the conclusion must follow logically from the premises. The next two examples will illustrate this point:

Example 1

If inflation increases, the mortgage rates will rise.
Inflation has increased.
Therefore, the mortgage rates will rise.

In this deductive argument, the premises (presuming that they are true) offer sufficient support for the conclusion to follow. Given the sufficient support of the premises in this argument, we cannot draw any other conclusion, except that the mortgage rates will rise.

Example 2

If you train for three hours a day, then you will be fit.
If you are fit, then you will do well in the upcoming marathon.
Therefore, if you train for three hours a day, then you will do well in the marathon.

In this inductive argument the premises, even if they were true, offer some support for the conclusion to follow, but the conclusion may be false. The conclusion does not follow logically from the premises, but only follows with probability.

We can also contrast deductive reasoning with inductive reasoning by pointing out that the connection between the premises and the conclusion of deductive arguments is narrow while, in the case of inductive reasoning, it is looser or more open-ended. Deductive reasoning works from broader generalisations or hypotheses to specific observations. Inductive reasoning moves from specific observations or situations to detecting patterns and then comes to general conclusions or generalisations. The following flow chart will illustrate the difference between deductive and inductive reasoning:

Deductive and Inductive Reasoning

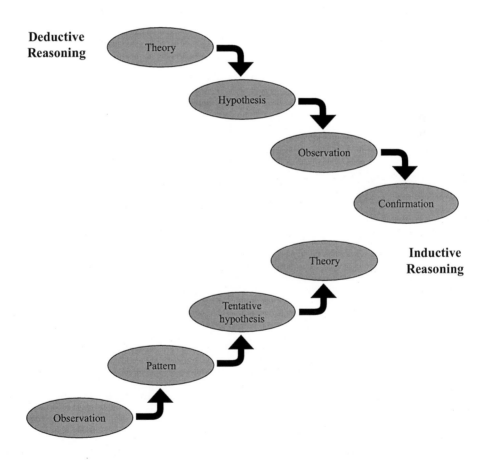

Exercise

Identify what type of argument appears in each of the following passages:

1. Hepatitis C is on the increase in South Africa's prison population. The spread of the disease is probably the result of inmates sharing needles. (Adapted from Teays 2003:245).

2. Elephants are emotionally similar to humans. They get distressed when they are separated from their families. They show strong emotions of grief when their young ones are taken away from them. Young bulls, when relocated to another reserve, even rebel and attack tourists. Often a matriarch elephant is sent to teach the young elephants to behave in appropriate ways. After they have been trained by the matriarch they settle down. Because elephants have the same strong emotions as humans, it follows that humans are obliged to act in a moral way towards them.

3. All rats are mammals. All mammals are warm-blooded. So, all rats are warm-blooded.

4. All birds can swim. All spotted eagle-owls are birds. So, all spotted eagle-owls can swim.

5. Sixty percent of people polled by KwaZulu-Natal disapprove of legalising active voluntary euthanasia. Thus, 60 percent of all South Africans disapprove of legalising active voluntary euthanasia.

6. Capital punishment is cruel. What is more, capital punishment is unworthy of a civilised society. Therefore, capital punishment is morally wrong.

7. The act of abortion is wrong. A fetus is a sentient being. Every sentient being deserves to live. Thus, the killing of a fetus is wrong.

Answers

1. This is an inductive empirical argument using cause-and-effect reasoning. It is claimed that inmates' sharing of needles in prisons causes the occurrence, the occurrence being the spread of Hepatitis C.

2. This is an inductive empirical argument using analogy. The argument rests on a comparison between elephants and human beings, and it is claimed that elephants and humans share a common feature, namely, strong emotions. On the basis of this it is then inferred that elephants probably share another common feature with humans, namely, moral worth.

3. This is a sound deductive empirical argument. The argument is valid and both the premises are true. The conclusion follows from the premises and the conclusion is also true.

4. This is an unsound deductive empirical argument. The argument is valid because the conclusion follows logically from the premises. However, the argument is not sound, because the first premise is false.

5. This is an example of an inductive empirical argument using statistical extrapolations. The argument uses statistical reasoning and draws on one sample study and then infers that all voters will vote against the legalising of active voluntary euthanasia.

6. This is an inductive value argument.

7. This is a deductive value argument.

8   Distinguishing good arguments from bad arguments

Formal logic concerns the structure and *validity* of arguments; the truth of the premises is assumed. In critical reasoning, though, we do not assume the truth of the premises of an argument. Critical reasoning goes further than merely clarifying the structure of arguments and establishing whether or not an argument is valid. Remember that an argument can be valid, but unsound. No critical thinker will accept an argument that is unsound. Critical reasoning is not only concerned with the validity, but also with the *soundness* of arguments: we critically examine the truth (or strength) of the premises of arguments. When we assess the soundness of an argument we want to establish whether or not the evidence provided by the premises is actually true or acceptable. When evaluating arguments our task as critical thinkers is to distinguish between good and bad reasoning. The following criteria serve as guidelines to distinguish between good and bad arguments:

1. A good argument is a *sound* argument. An argument is sound if good reason is given to believe the premises *and* if the premises adequately support the conclusion. On the other hand, an argument is poor when it is fallacious (see chapter 2), or when the reasons advanced are doubtful and do not sufficiently support the conclusion.

2. A good argument is an argument that is *consistent*. The premises of a consistent argument do not contradict each other. Contradictory premises cannot be a good reason for believing the conclusion. Let us take the following example:

    JANE: All suffering, whether it is human or animal suffering, is morally bad. Therefore, abortion is morally wrong.

    MIKE: My goodness, Jane! How can you claim that? You just ate a large juicy steak!

In this argument Mike is pointing out that Jane contradicts herself. Jane claims that abortion is morally wrong because all suffering is morally bad. Yet, at the same time, she has just enjoyed a steak, not thinking about the suffering of the animal that was killed to provide the steak. The reason Jane gave in support of her claim is *inconsistent* with other values Jane holds.

3. A good argument is an argument where the evidence or reasons given in support of the conclusion are *relevant* to the truth or acceptability of the conclusion. One way of distinguishing good arguments from bad ones is to establish whether the reasons an arguer advances in support of the conclusion are relevant. To establish whether a premise is relevant to a conclusion, assume that it is false and then decide whether this makes a difference to the truth of the conclusion. If it does not make a difference, then we can disregard that premise as irrelevant support of the conclusion. Here is an example:

> At a dinner party one of your friends claims that most people find cigarette smoking in public places offensive. You happen to be a smoker and you have just lit a cigarette at the dinner table. You oppose this view and point out that smokers have a right to smoke where they want and that if non-smokers find it offensive, then they should go somewhere else. As a student in critical reasoning you are curious, though, about the reasons for your friend's belief. You ask him why he thinks that most people find smoking in public places offensive. Your friend explains that leading academics agree with this. You question the evidence and point out that, even if it is true that leading academics agree with this, it is not at all obvious why it should be considered relevant to the truth of the claim that most people find cigarette smoking in public places offensive. Your friend explains that leading academics who have extensively investigated people's attitudes to cigarette smoking in public places all agree that most people find it offensive.

Do you think the reason your friend offers in support of his claim is relevant?

In my opinion, your friend has offered relevant evidence in support of his claim. The initial reason your friend offered in support of the claim that most people find smoking in public places offensive was incompletely expressed. You assumed the premise in support of the claim to be false and, as a critical thinker, you applied the principle of charitable interpretation (taking into consideration that more than one interpretation of an argument is possible) and challenged him to provide more evidence in support of his view. Your friend defended his position by trying to give stronger reasons in support of his claim. He then gave the following reason: leading academics *who have extensively investigated people's attitudes to cigarette smoking in public places* all agree that most people find it offensive. The evidence that is given in support of the claim is *relevant* and it makes a difference to the truth or validity of the conclusion.

4. In a good argument, the claims that are advanced in support of the conclusion are *compatible* with other claims we know are true. To test whether the claims made in an argument are compatible with other well-substantiated claims, we should check whether or not the claims contradict other claims we know are true. Read the following example:

> You should not shake hands or hug a friend who has AIDS, because you can be infected by bodily contact with someone who has AIDS.

This is a bad argument, because the reason offered in support of the conclusion is not compatible with established knowledge about HIV-infection.

It is a well-substantiated fact that the HIV virus can only be transmitted in the following ways: sexually; receiving HIV-infected blood; sharing needles; and transmission from a pregnant, HIV-positive woman to her fetus. In relation to this established knowledge, the claim that you can be infected by bodily contact with someone who has AIDS (for example, by shaking hands and hugging) clearly contradicts the knowledge we already have about AIDS.

In summary

In chapter 5 and in this chapter I explained some important aspects of argument evaluation. We have discussed the role of definitions, counterexamples and counterarguments. We have explored the difference between empirical and value arguments; we discussed deductive and inductive arguments; we emphasised that validity is not the same as soundness; and we noted some criteria to distinguish good arguments from bad ones. In the next chapter we will apply the knowledge and skills we have obtained to evaluate a number of arguments.

Applying your knowledge and skills to the evaluation of arguments

CHAPTER 7

The pure and the simple truth is rarely pure and never simple.

Oscar Wilde

n this chapter we will apply what we have learnt in the previous chapters to the evaluation of arguments. To help you understand and evaluate arguments, I will set out five steps in argument evaluation. Remember that these steps are only guidelines and are not meant to be followed blindly. There are many ways to evaluate arguments. As a critical thinker, you can use your own methods. There are, however, certain points we have to look out for when we evaluate arguments. These are highlighted in the following steps:

1 Five steps in the evaluation of arguments

1.1 *Understand the meaning of the argument*

Make sure that you understand what the argument is, in fact, saying – in other words, the meaning of the argument. Do not underestimate the importance of this step. The very first thing you need to establish is whether a passage does, in fact, present an argument, or whether it describes, explains, narrates or commands. If it is an argument, make sure you understand its meaning. If there are any words you do not understand, look them up in a good dictionary. If there are ambiguous words or phrases replace them with words or phrases that, in your opinion, clearly express the arguer's meaning. Remember to apply the principle of charitable interpretation here. There is no point in making an argument look silly just so that you can show it to be unsound. Give the arguer the benefit of the doubt and express the argument in its strongest possible form. This might mean that you have to read and reread the passage carefully several times before you understand it.

Keep in mind the context of the passage and consider key words and recurring themes. Decide whether there is one argument, or more – and, if so, how they are related. At this early stage of argument evaluation it is also important to determine what type of argument is being made, because different types of arguments are assessed differently. Determine whether the argument is deductive, inductive, empirical or a value argument. Remember that a single complex argument may include all four types.

1.2 Identify the main point of the argument

The next important thing to do is to find the main conclusion of the argument. It is not always easy to identify the main point of the argument, because the writing style may be obscure, or the main conclusion may not be explicitly stated. If you cannot establish the main point, or if you are unsure of what the arguer is claiming, you will not be able to formulate your arguments in support of or against the viewpoint advanced by the arguer. Although a complex argument may have several sub-arguments, each with its own conclusion, it is important to concentrate on the *main point* that states the single crucial issue in the argument. Remember that you might need to paraphrase or restate assertions made in the passage in order to draw out the implied conclusion and premises.

1.3 Locate the reasons that support the main point of the argument

After you have identified the main conclusion of the argument, the next logical step is to find the reasons (the premises) the arguer provides in support of the main point of her argument. As in the case of identifying the main conclusion of an argument, it may be difficult to find the premises that are offered in support of the conclusion. You will sometimes come across a text that is badly written or unclear. At other times you will deal with complex arguments, where the premises in support of the conclusion are sub-conclusions, supported by other premises. You may also come across arguments where the premises are not explicitly stated. In such cases you have to draw out the implied premises. Remember, however, that you cannot add premises randomly in order to ensure that the conclusion will follow. In chapter 3 we pointed out that the task of identifying implicit premises amounts to adding premises that are *needed* to support the conclusion; however, this does not mean that we are entitled to distort the meaning of the passage.

1.4 Determine whether the reasons offered in support of the conclusion are acceptable

Good arguments provide acceptable reasons in support of their conclusions. Remember that in chapter 2 we said that, whenever we give reasons in support of a claim, we are engaged in reasoning. However, it is one thing to give reasons to support a claim, and quite another to provide acceptable reasons. When we evaluate arguments, our task is to determine whether the reasons an argument advances for accepting its conclusion are acceptable. In chapter 6 we discussed some guidelines to distinguish between sound and faulty reasoning. If you have forgotten these guidelines, turn back to chapter six and read through the section on 'Distinguishing good arguments from bad arguments'. To decide whether the reasons advanced in accepting the conclusion of the argument are acceptable, we could also try to construct counterexamples and counterarguments (see chapter 5).

It is also helpful to evaluate the definitions (if any) in the argument. Determine what types of definitions (denotative, logical, stipulative or persuasive) are used, and whether they are acceptable. Lastly, check whether the argument is fallacious in any way and whether the arguer has based his or her claims on unexamined, preconceived ideas.

1.5 State your own opinion

Note that, even though an argument may be a good one, in the sense that the premises give sufficient support for the conclusion, you may still *disagree* with the arguer's viewpoint or perspective, in which case it is important to state your own views.

Giving your own opinion on the issue being debated is a sign of critical reflection. Of course, you must give reasons to support your viewpoint. Your reasons must be acceptable, appropriate and relevant. You may well find it useful to use examples to illustrate your point. You could also use this opportunity to suggest what could be done to improve the argument under discussion.

2 Testing your knowledge and skills in evaluating arguments

Here are a number of exercises. These exercises require you to apply the knowledge and skills you have gained so far to the evaluation of arguments.

Exercise

Critically evaluate the following arguments:

1. 'Over the past ten years, there has been a four-fold increase in the number of people killed in road accidents who are found to have illegal drugs in their bodies. The rate of increase is much greater than the corresponding figure for those people killed in accidents who were found with alcohol in their blood. This shows that the campaign against drink-driving has succeeded. Consequently, the government ought now to concentrate on targeting those people who drive whilst under the influence of illegal drugs.' (Fisher 2001:176)

2. 'Euthanasia cannot be justified. The judgement that a patient is terminally ill isn't always the last word, you know. The diagnosis may be mistaken, a new cure may come along, and cancer patients have been known to go into spontaneous remission. But death is the last word. Once you have killed a patient, he or she is beyond all hope. How would you feel if a wonder drug turned up the next day, or if the doctors discovered their diagnosis was wrong?' (Adapted from Olen & Barry 1999:235)

3. A minister of religion claims the following:

   Marriage is a sacred undertaking between a man and a woman. Therefore, a marriage commitment between same-sex partners undermines the holiness of marriage.

4. 'Most parents want their children to have successful careers. Since education is essential to success, it is the duty of parents to give children the best possible education. Because it is also in the country's economic interest to have a highly educated population, the government should help parents to provide for their children's education. Therefore all parents should receive financial help towards the cost of their children's education, so the low paid should receive tax credits and those who are better off should receive tax relief.' (Fisher 2001:24)

5. PAMELA: For goodness sake, Sam! Why do you throw your rubbish out of the window? Don't you know that littering is harmful to the environment? If we all do what you are doing, then soon our world will be such a messy place that not even a rat would like to live in it.

   SAM: What are you talking about? Of course I must throw my rubbish around. Didn't you know that littering is acceptable, because it creates jobs for people?

6. 'Whatever goes on between consenting adults in private is nobody's business but their own, and that holds for sex as much as for anything else. Why should anybody even care whether Mary has fifteen lovers or none, whether Jack

prefers sex with Bill to sex with Jane, or whether married couples like to 'swing' with other married couples? Just because you personally disapprove of such things doesn't make them wrong. We all have the right to live our lives as we see fit as long as we don't interfere with the rights of others to live their lives as they see fit. Promiscuous people, homosexuals, and swingers don't tell you how to live your life. Don't tell them how to live theirs.' (Olen & Barry 1999:82)

7. 'More than 2000 years after Plato first raised the problem of social justice, modern philosophers continue to quarrel over what it means to say of a society that it is just or unjust. It is pointless to argue about the issue of social justice. If there has been no progress after 2000 years then the prospect for progress in the next 2000 years is zero.'

8. 'Abortion is morally justified on the grounds that the rights and wellbeing of the mother override those of the fetus. The mother is a rational and moral agent, whereas it cannot be claimed that the fetus has rational capacity or that it is a moral agent. When we need to decide whether or not to abort a fetus, it is thus reasonable to say that the mother has the right to decide whether or not to abort. Furthermore, should we give precedence to the so-called right to life of unborn fetuses, then this decision will have devastating consequences for children, mothers and society. Some of the consequences include: thousands of unwanted children who would probably become street children; more people dying of starvation; and women powerless to decide about their own bodies and their own wellbeing.'

9. 'Your views have led to a number of crazy consequences. I'm not just talking about such tragedies as teen mothers, but things like the gay rights movement. First we have homosexuals demanding the right to teach in elementary schools, then we have homosexual couples demanding the right to adopt children, then we have them demanding that homosexual "spouses" be included in family medical plans and the like. I have no idea where all this is ultimately heading, but it's certainly not in the right direction. We can't let children grow up believing that homosexuality is just another lifestyle, and we can't have society treating homosexual relationships like real marriages. No society can survive that.' (Olen & Barry 1999:85)

> **Note:** In example (9), when the arguer talks about 'your views', he is referring to someone who is in favour of the law allowing people to adopt a specific sexual lifestyle.

10. 'Psychiatric records, including even the identification of a person as a patient, must be protected with extreme care. Confidentiality is essential to psychiatric treatment. This is based in part on the special nature of psychiatric therapy as well as on the traditional ethical relationship between physician and patient. Growing concern regarding the civil rights of patients and the possible adverse

effects of computerisation, duplication equipment, and data banks makes the dissemination of confidential information an increasing hazard. Because of the sensitive and private nature of the information with which the psychiatrist deals, he/she must be circumspect about the information that he/she chooses to disclose to others about a patient. The welfare of the patient must be a continuing consideration.' (Freeman 1999:304)

11.

Court put on hold hearing on Zuma charges

The Democratic Alliance's urgent application to overturn the National Prosecuting Authority's decision to withdraw criminal charges against President Jacob Zuma was postponed indefinitely in the High Court in Pretoria on Tuesday.

Following an agreement between the parties, Judge Francis Legodi granted an order setting down time frames for the filing of further affidavits in a number of interlocutory applications which are to precede the DA's main application.

These will include an application by Zuma's lawyers against the DA for security for costs, which will probably only be heard early in August.

Time frames were also laid down for the filing of further court papers in an application by defence contractor Dr Richard Young to intervene as a party to the application, and in the DA's application to force the NPA to hand over documents which led to its controversial April 2009 decision.

Zuma has not been acquitted

The documents sought by the DA exclude confidential submissions Zuma made to the NPA.

Papers in these applications will have to be filed by August 21, after which they will be set down for hearing as soon as possible.

The DA filed the application for a judicial review of the decision to withdraw fraud, corruption, racketeering and money laundering charges against Zuma early in April.

DA leader Helen Zille maintained that the NPA decision was 'political stage management disguised as legal procedure' and that the NPA had caved in to political pressure and had 'thrown the law-book out of the window'.

Zuma has not been acquitted. Only a court of law can do that. Only a court of law can examine and cross-examine the evidence that the [National Director of Public Prosecutions] submitted in mitigation of the decision to drop the charges.

And only a court of law can determine whether the decision itself was lawful or not.

'The DA believes a judicial review is the only way to ensure that justice takes it course,' she said at the time.

The DA contended in court papers that the decision was not rational and was in fact unlawful and unconstitutional.

The NPA has maintained that the DA did not have the legal standing to bring the application and that the decision not to prosecute Zuma was not reviewable. - *Sapa*

(Published on the Web by *Independent Online* on 2009-06-09, 17:09:49)

12.

Going nowhere: Zimbabwe will only recover when Robert Mugabe goes

It's still there, and just as bad as ever. The outside world has all but forgotten Zimbabwe, where Robert Mugabe continues the preside over economic and political collapse. But the southern African country is making miserable milestones by day. Four out of five adults are now unemployed. Zimbabwe suffers the world's highest inflation rate, a stratospheric 1,600%. Toilet paper is more valuable than bank notes. The price of bread (when it's available) more than doubled in January; mealie meal, a staple, rose by 500% last week.

Price freezes mean that basics, like milk and sugar, are rarely available. Many recent printed bank notes have not been issued because they are worthless. Roughly 3m people, by some estimates, have fled the country, leaving about 12m behind. On Monday February 19th the European Union – to little fanfare – agreed to renew 'smart' sanctions, including an arms embargo and travel ban for Zimbabwe's leadership, that have been in place for years.

The cause of Zimbabwe's collapse, ultimately, is Mr Mugabe's refusal to leave office. Increasingly under pressure from unhappy Zimbabweans, he has lashed out at an array of enemies, including black opposition leaders, white farmers, trade unions, women's groups, urban voters and Britain – the former colonial power. By seizing commercial farms and handing them to political cronies, Mr Mugabe may have staved off the end of his political career, but at the cost of ruining an economy dominated by agriculture. Aid and investment have dried up.

Manufacturing has slumped.

The prolonged economic collapse is more typical of a country wrecked by war. The purchasing power of the average Zimbabwean today, for example, is back at levels last seen soon after the Second World War, according to the Centre for Global Development, a think-tank in Washington, DC. Given widespread AIDS and hunger, this translates into thousands of unnecessary deaths each year.

When will anything be done about it? Weary analysts have stopped trying to predict how far the economy will have to collapse, or for oppression to worsen, before something snaps. But even leaders in the ruling ZANU-PF party know that recovery depends on getting the old crocodile out of office. Investors, farmers, refugees, tourists and others will not return while Mr Mugabe's misrule continues. Yet managing his exit is proving impossible.

Rival camps in the ruling party are vying for eventual control, so nobody dares push the chief to go. (Indeed Mr Mugabe may be dividing his allies for precisely this reason). The army is watching suspiciously. The big neighbour – South Africa – is reluctant to get involved, fearing that any intervention may backfire. The opposition, deflated after seeing general elections rigged and its supporters crushed, has become timid and divided. Many of the brightest and bravest, in any case, are moving abroad. Nor are sustained street protests likely, though there are occasional signs of violence in the townships around the capital, Harare. Strikes are becoming more common.

At the weekend heavily armed riot police in Harare crushed an opposition rally – despite High Court approval for it to go ahead – by firing teargas and using water cannon. Protesters responded by throwing stones. Over 120 people were arrested.

This week, to mark his birthday, Mr Mugabe will have a lavish party, to which teachers and nurses have been forced to contribute. He will also give a speech in which he is expected to mention his succession. Officially, after nearly three decades in office, he is supposed to go in March 2008. But a presidential election scheduled for that month may well be postponed for another two years, when he will be 86. In any case he has told foreign journalists, perhaps in jest, that he plans to rule until he is 'a century old'.

Is anything like that dismal prospect possible? Mr Mugabe is relatively healthy and alert, and has the tacit support of both other African countries and of China, which is asserting itself on the continent. And though outsiders occasionally grumble about the misery in Zimbabwe – America has called it an 'outpost of tyranny' – the West has broadly decided that ignoring Mr Mugabe is the least bad strategy. Any change, therefore, is going to have to come from within. And, so far, Mr Mugabe has proved a master at stamping that out.

(From Economist.com, 2007-02-20)

13.
Darfur Crimes against Humanity and International Failure

Nassim, Damascus: 2008-12-09

The massacres continue in Sudan in the Darfur region by the criminal regime of Omar Hassan al-Bashir, who has proved that he is no less than a world-class criminal against humanity.

In addition to widespread killing and ethnic cleansing by the criminal al-Bashir and his criminal subjects of some tribes in the region like 'Janjaweed' working and killing under the direct command of al-Bashir, Darfur is suffering a wide range of unbelievable human rights violations and atrocities by which a comprehensive system of deprivation, humiliation and torture is imposed on the indigenous population of Darfur of non-Arab origin.

This system is comprehensive to the letter in that it targets every single human right and living means of the indigenous population of Darfur. This comprehensive system of crimes against humanity includes everything from food and water deprivation to systematic rape, besides direct killing of course.

The criminal al-Bashir, besides his regime and subject criminals of militants and tribesmen, made really an exceptional system of human rights violations and atrocities along with ethnic cleansing, which is definitely worthy of historical archiving and citation as a moment in which the humanity failed in defending itself.

This continued tragic situation in Darfur somehow reflects the repeated failure of the international order to maintain peace and security and to save human dignity and basic human rights, especially as regards the question of Darfur in Sudan so far. This repeated and somehow familiar international failure has not been significantly changed even after the end of the Cold War and the dismantling of the totalitarian Eastern Campaign.

Apart from this international failure, there was an international shy but significant step represented by the hardly taken resolution by the UN Security Council about referring the crimes against humanity committed in Darfur to the International Criminal Court (ICC).

In this regard, the judicial authorities of the ICC, which have shown seriousness and clear and steady commitment to justice so far besides an indifference to politics and political distortion, and deserve a tribute in this regard, might compensate the international failure at the political level in achieving peace and security for the victim civilian population of Darfur.

Hence, it is a humanitarian responsibility upon all parties to support the work of the International Criminal Court in the Darfur case to achieve justice there, as a way leading to peace and security for the long-time suffering civilian population of Darfur.

(From http://liberator.instablogs.com 2008-12-09)

14.

South Africa Race Relations – South Africa

Race relations and the remnants of Apartheid in South Africa are so complex and deeply rooted that trying to make sense of it can make your head spin at times. During a road trip through the Eastern Cape, I saw so many different sides to the country – a lunch with black revolutionary Steve Biko's widow and a two-day stay with white Afrikaner farmers in the rural countryside – that I wasn't sure how I felt about both the past and future of South Africa.

Our afternoon with Mrs Biko was inspiring. We visited her husband's grave, where she spoke of the contributions he had made to end Apartheid in South Africa and to raise black consciousness. She allowed us to tour the business center she had set up for black South Africans, where people could receive help with resumés and obtain access to computers and fax machines.

Only a day later, we were in home-stays on Afrikaner farms, where black male workers were still referred to as 'boys' and dogs were trained to attack anyone who was not white. How could this be the same South Africa? Were things really getting better or had not much changed in the 11 years since the end of Apartheid?

We quickly learnt that things were not as simple or easy as they first appeared. Some people still held the same views they had before Apartheid ended, making race relations tense. Some people had managed to forgive the atrocities they had endured because they believed in a better future for their country. Many blacks were still living in poverty in townships; many white Afrikaners were facing huge financial hardship after losing farms that had been in their families for generations. Some blacks were using new advantages to leave the townships and gain education and money; some whites continued to live in the sprawling mansions in gated communities just as they had during Apartheid. Things were better, things were worse, things were the same. How do you make any sense of it?

I think understanding that relations in South Africa remain complicated is a sure way to help understand the country you are encountering. Talk to people wherever you go, and make an effort to engage with people from all different backgrounds – blacks, whites, coloureds, Xhosa, Cape Malays, Afrikaners. You will encounter them all in Cape Town.

I also found it useful and interesting to do a variety of reading before I left for Cape Town. A simple understanding of Cape Town's history, from the San people to Jan van Riebeeck to Steve Biko, is useful, as is reading literature from South Africa authors. I would enthusiastically recommend JM Coetzee (particularly *Disgrace*) or Nadine Gordimer – both are internationally popular and respected South African authors who paint a picture of what race relations in South Africa have been like, spawning about 30 years. It wouldn't be a bad idea to read beloved former president Nelson Mandela's autobiography *Long walk to freedom*, as nearly every South African you will meet has read it, or Archbishop Desmond Tutu's book *No future without forgiveness* which deals with South Africa's Truth and Reconciliation Commission.

> South Africa has a confusing, painful and intense past – which a majority of Capetonians will tell you makes the present and the future all the more rich and interesting. How they deal with relations seems to be a glimpse at humanity, or at the very least, real human beings.
>
> (From http://www.bootsnall.com/articles 2005-11-18)

Answers

I will provide answers to activities (2), (4), (7) and (9). Apply the knowledge you have gained from the previous exercises and complete exercises (1), (3), (5), (6), (8), (10), (11), (12), (13) and (14) on your own.

At the outset we need to remember the steps involved in the evaluation of arguments. Here is a summary of these steps:

1. What kind of argument are we dealing with?
2. What is the arguer claiming?
3. What reasons does the arguer offer to support his claim?
4. Are the reasons in support of the conclusion acceptable?
5. Is it a good argument? Give reasons for your answer.

Activity (2)

Euthanasia cannot be justified. The judgement that a patient is terminally ill isn't always the last word, you know. The diagnosis may be mistaken, a new cure may come along, and cancer patients have been known to go into spontaneous remission. But death is the last word. Once you have killed a patient, he or she is beyond all hope. How would you feel if a wonder drug turned up the next day, or if the doctors discovered their diagnosis was wrong?

First we need to analyse the argument to reveal its structure. Once you are more experienced in argument evaluation, you will find that it is not always necessary to analyse the argument first. With practice you will, after carefully reading the text, immediately spot the conclusion and premises of the argument. For now, I will analyse the argument to determine the conclusion(s) and premises:

[Euthanasia cannot be justified][1]. [The judgement that a patient is terminally ill isn't always the last word][2], you know. [The diagnosis may be mistaken][3], [a new cure may come along][4], and [cancer patients have been known to go into spontaneous remission][5]. But [death is the last word][6]. [Once you have killed a patient, he or she is beyond all hope][7]. How would you feel if a wonder drug turned up the next day, or if the doctors discovered their diagnosis was wrong?

> Chain argument (There are two conclusions in the argument)
> Main conclusion – 1
> Premises for main conclusion – 2, 3, 4, 5, 6
> Sub-conclusion – 6
> Premise for sub-conclusion – 7

1. This is an inductive value argument.

2. The arguer is claiming that euthanasia cannot be justified. Note that there is also a sub-conclusion, which claims that death is the last word.

3. (a) The arguer gives the following reasons to support the main conclusion:

   (i) The judgement that a patient is terminally ill isn't always the last word.

   (ii) The diagnosis may be mistaken.

   (iii) A new cure may come along.

   (iv) Cancer patients have been known to go into spontaneous remission.

   (b) The following reason is given in support of the sub-conclusion:

   (i) Once you have killed a patient, he or she is beyond all hope.

   Note that the sentence at the end of the passage, 'How would you feel if a wonder drug turned up the next day, or if the doctors discovered their diagnosis was wrong?', is not a statement, but a question. It does not give any support to the conclusion and the arguer could have left it out.

4. A good way to establish whether the premises of the argument are acceptable is to find counterexamples and counterarguments to the arguer's statements.

   (a) Let us examine whether the premises the arguer offers in support of his main conclusion are acceptable. The main conclusion is: 'Euthanasia cannot be justified'.

   (i) The statement, 'The judgement that a patient is terminally ill isn't always the last word', does not really say anything new – it only restates the second premise, 'The diagnosis may be mistaken'.

   (ii) The plausibility of the statement, 'The diagnosis may be mistaken', is questionable. From experience and previous knowledge we know that medical specialists seldom make mistakes when diagnosing terminal cancer. Moreover, a second opinion is usually asked before a final diagnosis is reached. This premise does not adequately support the conclusion.

(iii) The statement, 'A new cure may come along', is not acceptable. The following counterexample can be used to refute the arguer's claim: it could take years before a new cure for terminal cancer is found, if at all. Again, the premise does not adequately support the conclusion.

(iv) The statement, 'Cancer patients have been known to go into spontaneous remission', is equally doubtful. Very few cancer patients have ever gone into spontaneous remission. The premise does not adequately support the conclusion.

(b) Is the premise the arguer gives in support of the sub-conclusion of the argument acceptable? The sub-conclusion is: 'Death is the last word'.

(i) The statement, 'Once you have killed a patient, he or she is beyond all hope', is just a repetition of what was stated in the sub-conclusion. The premise does not support the sub-conclusion.

5. This is a bad argument for the following reasons:

(i) The argument is *not sound* because the arguer fails to offer good reasons in support of what he or she is claiming.

(ii) None of the premises adequately supports the conclusions of the argument. This means that the truth of the claim that euthanasia cannot be justified is disputable.

(iii) The arguer does not give a *definition* of the term 'euthanasia'. What type of euthanasia is the arguer talking about? Is it active voluntary euthanasia, active involuntary euthanasia, passive voluntary euthanasia, or passive involuntary euthanasia? *Active voluntary euthanasia* occurs when a competent adult patient requests or gives explicit consent to certain medical treatment or non-treatment. In some cases of active voluntary euthanasia, the patient requests that he or she be given a lethal injection. *Active involuntary euthanasia* occurs where a patient is competent to make decisions, does not consent or request euthanasia, but a third person, out of pity or for whatever reason, decides to perform euthanasia on the patient by, for instance, administering a fatal drug overdose. *Passive voluntary euthanasia* occurs when a patient chooses to die by refusing treatment, or instructs others to act on his or her behalf. For instance, a terminally ill patient can appoint the spouse, family or a lawyer as proxy decision-maker to cease life-sustaining treatment in the event that he or she is incapable of doing so. *Passive involuntary euthanasia* refers to cases of euthanasia where the decision is not made by the person whose life is at issue, but by others. These cases include situations where patients are incompetent to give informed consent to life-or-death decisions and others, usually the family, make important decisions for them. A value judgement such as 'euthanasia is wrong' is too generalised because, in deciding whether euthanasia is morally (or legally) justified, we have to know which type of euthanasia we are dealing with.

Activity (4)

Most parents want their children to have successful careers. Since education is essential to success, it is the duty of parents to give children the best possible education. Because it is also in the country's economic interest to have a highly educated population, the government should help parents to provide for their children's education. Therefore all parents should receive financial help towards the cost of their children's education, so the low paid should receive tax credits and those who are better off should receive tax relief.

Turn to Exercise 1 in section 5 of chapter four. Here we analysed this complex argument to reveal its structure. We presented its structure as follows:

[Most parents want their children to have successful careers][1]. *Since* [education is essential to success][2], [it is the duty of parents to give children the best possible education][3]. *Because* [it is also in the country's economic interest to have a highly educated population][4], [the government should help parents to provide for their children's education][5]. *Therefore* [all parents should receive financial help towards the cost of their children's education][6], *so* [the low paid should receive tax credits and those who are better off should receive tax relief][7].

Chain argument (There are four conclusions in the argument)

Main conclusion – 7
Premise for main conclusion – 6
Sub-conclusion – 6
Premise for sub-conclusion – 5
Sub-conclusion – 5
Premises for sub-conclusion – 3, 4
Sub-conclusion – 3
Premises for sub-conclusion – 1, 2

In evaluating this argument, I will help you to establish what kind of argument it is, what the arguer is claiming and what reasons the arguer offers in support of his or her claims. You should complete the evaluation of this argument on your own by applying the experience you have gained from the previous example to answer the following questions:

- Are the reasons in support of the conclusions acceptable?
- Is it a good argument? Give reasons for your answer.

1. The kind of argument we are dealing with here is an inductive empirical argument.

2. In this chain argument the arguer makes four claims, one main claim (the main conclusion) and three sub-claims (sub-conclusions).

The main conclusion (the point the arguer is trying to convince us of) is:

- The low paid should receive tax credits and those who are better off should receive tax relief. (statement number 7)

The first sub-conclusion is:

- All parents should receive financial help towards the cost of their children's education. (statement number 6)

The second sub-conclusion is:

- The government should help parents to provide for their children's education. (statement number 5)

The third sub-conclusion is:

- It is the duty of parents to give children the best possible education. (statement number 3)

3. What reasons does the arguer give to support his or her claims?
    (a) The arguer gives the following reason is support of the main conclusion:
        (i) All parents should receive financial help towards the cost of their children's education. (statement number 6)
    (b) The following reason is offered in support of the first sub-conclusion:
        (i) The government should help parents to provide for their children's education. (statement number 5)
    (c) The following reasons are given in support of the second sub-conclusion:
        (i) It is the duty of parents to give children the best possible education. (statement number 3)
        (ii) It is in the country's economic interest to have a highly educated population. (statement number 4).
    (d) The arguer gives the following reasons for the third sub-conclusion:
        (i) Most parents want their children to have successful careers. (statement number 1)
        (ii) Education is essential to success. (statement number 2)

Activity (7)

More than 2 000 years after Plato first raised the problem of social justice, modern philosophers continue to quarrel over what it means to say of a society that it is just or unjust. It is pointless to argue about the issue of social justice. If there has been no progress after 2 000 years then the prospect for progress in the next 2 000 years is zero.

1. This is an inductive value argument.

2. The arguer of this passage is claiming that there is no point in arguing about the problem of social justice, because 2 000 years after Plato first raised the issue of social justice, philosophers have made no progress in solving the problem. The arguer then infers that, because philosophers have quarrelled for 2 000 years, without reaching consensus, over what it means to say that a society is just or unjust, they will not make any progress solving the issue in the next 2 000 years.

3. The reasons the arguer gives in support of the conclusion can be determined by analysing the argument as follows:

    [More than 2 000 years after Plato first raised the problem of social justice, modern philosophers continue to quarrel over what it means to say of a society that it is just or unjust][1]. [It is pointless to argue about the issue of social justice][2]. [If there has been no progress after 2 000 years, then the prospect for progress in the next 2000 years is zero][3].

Conclusion – 2
Premises – 1 and 3

The reasons offered in support of the conclusion are the following:

(i)   More than 2 000 years after Plato first raised the problem of social justice, modern philosophers continue to quarrel over what it means to say of a society that it is just or unjust.

(ii) If there has been no progress after 2000 years, then the prospect for progress in the next 2000 years is zero.

4. The reasons offered in support of the conclusion are not acceptable. A number of counterarguments can be given, as I have done in point (5) below, to refute the arguer's statements.

5. In my opinion, it is a bad argument for the following reasons:

(i)   The argument is based on the assumption that debating problems concerning values is pointless, while simultaneously making a value judgement. Note that the arguer *himself* makes a value judgement. This kind of reasoning is *inconsistent and unreasonable*.

(ii)   The arguer does not take into account that the problem of social justice has to do with values. Our values determine the judgements we make about social justice. Because values differ from individual to individual and from culture to culture, it is difficult, if not impossible, to reach agreement on value issues. This is the reason why philosophers disagree about what it means to say that a society is just or unjust.

(iii) The fact that we do not agree on the meaning of 'social justice' and its application to real-life situations does not imply that debating the problem is pointless.

Activity (9)

Your views have led to a number of crazy consequences. I'm not just talking about such tragedies as teen mothers, but things like the gay rights movement. First we have homosexuals demanding the right to teach in elementary schools, then we have homosexual couples demanding the right to adopt children, then we have them demanding that homosexual 'spouses' be included in family medical plans and the like. I have no idea where all this is ultimately heading, but it's certainly not in the right direction. We can't let children grow up believing that homosexuality is just another lifestyle, and we can't have society treating homosexual relationships like real marriages. No society can survive that.

1.   This is an inductive value argument.

2.   The arguer is claiming that no society can survive homosexuality as a form of sexual choice, because we can't let children grow up believing that homosexuality is just another lifestyle, and we can't have society treating homosexual relationships like real marriages.

3.   We can analyse the argument as follows:

> [Your views have led to a number of crazy consequences]^1. [I'm not just talking about such tragedies as teen mothers]^2, but [I'm talking about things like the gay rights movement]^3. *First* [we have homosexuals demanding the right to teach in elementary schools]^4, *then* [we have homosexual couples demanding the right to adopt children]^5, *then* [we have them demanding that homosexual 'spouses' be included in family medical plans and the like]^6. [I have no idea where all this is ultimately heading]^7, but [it's certainly not in the right direction]^8. [We can't let children grow up believing that homosexuality is just another lifestyle]^9, and [we can't have society treating homosexual relationships like real marriages]^{10}. [No society can survive that]^{11}.

Conclusion – 11

Premises for the conclusion – 1, 2, 3, 4, 5, 6, 7, 8, 9, 10

The reasons the arguer offers in support of the conclusion are the following:

(i)   Views on sexual liberty, including homosexuality, have led to a number of crazy consequences.

(ii)   When considering sexual liberty, the arguer does not only have in mind such tragedies as teen mothers.

(iii) He also has in mind the gay rights movement.

(iv) Homosexuals have demanded the right to teach in elementary schools.

(v)   Homosexual couples have demanded the right to adopt children.

(vi) It was demanded that homosexual 'spouses' be included in family medical plans and the like.

(vii) It is uncertain where all this is ultimately heading.

(viii) The arguer is convinced that it is not heading in the right direction.

(ix) Children cannot grow up believing that homosexuality is just another lifestyle.

(x)   We can't have society treating homosexual relationships like real marriages.

4.   The reasons offered in support of the conclusion are not acceptable. They do not *persuade* me to believe that homosexuality will destroy society. The arguer himself makes a value judgement, which is based on the *preconceived idea* that only heterosexual relationships are morally and legally acceptable.

5.   This is a bad argument for the following reasons:

(i)   The argument is fallacious because the reasons given are disputable and based on *preconceived ideas* about what kind of sexuality should count as moral and legal. What is moral about heterosexual relationships and what is immoral about homosexual relationships?

(ii)   The argument is guilty of presenting a *slippery slope fallacy* (see chapter 2). The arguer reasons in a chain with conditionals, and our attention is distracted by the thought of how terrible the situation would be if we allow homosexual relationships the same status, morally and legally, as heterosexual marriages. The slippery slope fallacy in this argument goes as follows: if we allow homosexuals the right to teach in elementary schools, and if we allow homosexual couples the right to adopt children, and if we allow homosexual spouses to be included in family medical plans, then something horrible will happen – we will end up raising an entire generation of homosexual children. This is unrealistic and an absurd claim.

3   The margin note and summary method of evaluating extended arguments

In the previous section we evaluated arguments by first analysing them to determine the conclusion(s) and the premises. We then applied the steps in argument evaluation to appraise the arguments. The arguments in the previous section were relatively short. When we have to evaluate *extended arguments*, however, this method is cumbersome and time-consuming. Here I want to introduce you to a much shorter way of evaluating arguments. It is a method Howard Kahane and Nancy Cavender use in their book *Logic and contemporary rhetoric* (2006:181–184). The advantage of this method is that it saves you time because you do not have to first analyse the argument and then rewrite all the premises and conclusions from the longer passage. This method is called *the margin note and summary method*.

There are four basic steps when using the *margin note and summary method:*

1.   Read the passage carefully and make sure you understand the meaning of the argument.

2.   Read the material again, this time marking or highlighting the important issues that are relevant to the argument.

3.   Use the margin on the right-hand side of the passage and make a brief summary of the passage, showing which statements are conclusions and which premises, so that the structure of the argument is 'lifted out'. The summary of the passage (the margin notes) need not be full sentences and you may use shorthand notes. Take care, however, that your summary is *accurate*, in other words, that it is a true reflection of what the writer is actually claiming – do not leave relevant points out and, at the same time, do not put words in the writer's mouth and thereby commit the straw man fallacy.

4.   Use your summary instead of the longer passage to evaluate the argument.

Let us now apply the margin note and summary method to evaluate the following passage:

Local leaders 'behind xenophobic attacks'

A report on xenophobic attacks, entitled *Towards Tolerance, Law and Dignity: Addressing Violence against Foreign Nationals in South Africa*, was commissioned by the International Organisation of Migration. It examined incidents of xenophobic violence between January 2007 and June 2008 across seven sites in Gauteng and the Western Cape. Respondents included township residents, non-nationals, community leaders, government officials, police and civil society.

The study found little evidence to support claims that a 'third force', poor border control, changes in political leadership or rising food and commodity prices caused the outbreak of xenophobic violence.

Researchers found that the violence is rooted in the 'micro politics' of South African townships and informal settlements. Sixty-two people, including 21 South Africans, were killed in the attacks and more than 150 000 were displaced.

The report has established that most of the violence was organised by local leaders and groups who wanted to further their own political and economic interests.

Conclusion
Most of the xenophobic violence was organised by local leaders and groups.

The report slammed local leaders and authorities, saying that 'community leaders and the local government did nothing to prevent or stop the violence'.

1. Community leaders and local authorities did nothing to prevent or stop the violence.

Instead, the study found that some were directly involved in the attacks, while others were reluctant to assist foreigners for fear of losing legitimacy or positions in the 2009 elections.

2. Some community leaders and local authorities were directly involved in the xenophobic attacks for fear of losing their positions in the 2009 elections.

Respondents were critical of the police, saying they were delayed and ineffective in dealing with the attacks. Many were convinced that some police officers supported or at least passively tolerated the violence due to their own anti-foreigner sentiments.

3. The police were ineffective in dealing with the attacks and passively tolerated the violence.

Reasons in support of the conclusion

The report warns against political leaders making spurious claims about foreigners that incite xenophobic attacks. It highlights the danger of political parties campaigning on an anti-foreigner ticket, which serves only to exacerbate some South African's prejudice against non-nationals.

The study emphasised the need for further and continuous research into anti-immigrant violence, and called on the media to be accurate and responsible in its reporting of migrants and migration.

(Adapted from *Mail & Guardian*, March 11 2009, 14:56)

Here is a summary of the extended argument on xenophobic violence, based on the margin notes:

Conclusion

Most of the violence was organised by local leaders and groups who wanted to further their own political and economic interests.

Reasons in support of the conclusion

1. Community leaders and local authorities did nothing to prevent or stop the violence.
2. Some community leaders and local authorities were directly involved in the xenophobic attacks for fear of losing their positions in the 2009 elections.
3. The police were ineffective in dealing with the attacks and passively tolerated the violence.

We will now use the summary, rather than working from the longer passage, to give a brief evaluation of the argument.

This is an inductive empirical argument. The claim that most of the violence was organised by local leaders and groups is based on evidence found by the study that can be empirically tested, that is, it can be verified or falsified by empirically determinable facts. The claim is inductive because the arguer infers something beyond what is stated in the premises. In a certain sense it is a good argument because the writer offers evidence or reasons in support his claim. Also, the arguer does not commit any fallacies of reasoning, such as the *ad hominem* fallacy or the straw man fallacy. In another sense it is a bad argument because the writer claims that no single factor could be isolated as the cause of the xenophobic attacks, which casts doubt on the accuracy of the study conducted to examine incidents of xenophobic violence between January 2007 and June 2008 across seven sites in Gauteng and the Western Cape.

Exercises

1. Take any textbook and select an extended argument from it. The textbook could be on philosophy, psychology, development studies, history, sociology, health care, and so on. Now evaluate the extended argument that you have selected by using the margin note and summary method.

2. Evaluate the following extended argument on the war in Afghanistan by using the margin note and summary method:

Voters turn against war in Afghanistan

Majority thinks conflict is unwinnable and wants troops withdrawn, poll shows

By Nigel Morris and Kim Sengupta
Tuesday, 28 July 2009

A majority of the public believes that the war in Afghanistan is unwinnable and British troops should be pulled out immediately, a poll for *The Independent* has found.

The growing opposition to the military offensive emerged as another two UK soldiers were killed, bringing the number of deaths so far this month to 22. Gordon Brown declared yesterday that Operation Panther's Claw – the five-week onslaught on Taliban positions in Helmand province – had been a success.

But today's ComRes survey suggests that the public mood is switching rapidly against the war – and that people do not believe it is worth sending reinforcements to Afghanistan.

More than half of voters (52 per cent) want troops to be withdrawn from Afghanistan straight away, with 43 per cent disagreeing. Opposition to the military action is even stronger among women.

By a margin of nearly two to one, the public believes that the Taliban cannot be defeated militarily. Fifty-eight per cent view the war as 'unwinnable', with 31 per cent disagreeing.

There is overwhelming agreement – by 75 per cent to 16 per cent – that British troops in Afghanistan lack the equipment they require to perform their role safely.

Despite that, 60 per cent of people do not think more troops and resources should be dispatched to the war zone. Just over one third (35 per cent) are in favour of reinforcements being sent in.

The collapse in confidence in Britain's involvement in Afghanistan comes after the numbers killed in the action exceeded those who died in Iraq.

Mr Brown yesterday announced the first phase of Panther's Claw had been a success, clearing out Taliban insurgents from a wide area of Helmand ahead of next month's Afghanistan elections.

He acknowledged the 'tragic human cost' among UK troops who were killed or injured, but insisted it had not been in vain. 'What we have actually done is make land secure for about 100,000 people', the Prime Minister claimed.

'What we've done is push back the Taliban – and what we've done also is to start to break that chain of terror that links the mountains of Afghanistan and Pakistan to the streets of Britain.'

The two latest deaths brought the total number of UK fatalities in Afghanistan to 191 since the invasion of 2001. One soldier, from the Light Dragoons, died while on a vehicle patrol in Lashkar Gah, the capital of Helmand. It was the first death in Operation Panther's Claw's second stage, which will focus on holding ground won from the Taliban in recent weeks. The second, from 5th Regiment Royal Artillery, died on foot patrol in Sangin district.

The American commander of Nato forces in Afghanistan, General Stanley McChrystal, is due to present his strategic plan for the campaign this week, emphasising that territory taken from the Taliban must be held. In the past, Western troops have been forced to abandon positions due to lack of numbers, allowing the insurgents to return.

For British troops the immediate effect of this is that they must now be present on the ground in large numbers in the areas they have captured. However, senior officers point out it also means that UK forces will not be able to mount such an operation on their own in the future without reinforcements, because troops will be tied up guarding the newly secured areas.

Lt-Gen Simon Mayall, deputy chief of the Defence Staff (Operations), declared: 'We cannot afford another Musa Qala.' He was referring to the capture of the Helmand town by British troops, who then withdrew after arriving at a deal with local elders. The area turned into an insurgent stronghold from which attacks were planned throughout southern Afghanistan.

Brigadier Tim Radford, who commanded the British troops in Panther's Claw, said: 'I am absolutely certain the operation has been a success. We've had a significant impact on the Taliban in this area – both in terms of their capability and their morale. It has been a very, very hard fight.

'When I have been on the ground, you look into the eyes of some of the soldiers and they have certainly grown up during this period.'

He refused to confirm how many insurgents were killed in the operation. But he said: 'There will be many Taliban who will not be fighting any more.'

Ministers are now backing moves by the Afghan government to draw moderate Taliban fighters into the political process by dividing them from hardcore militants.

David Miliband, the Foreign Secretary, speaking at Nato's headquarters in Brussels, said: 'The Afghan government needs effective grassroots initiatives to offer an alternative to fight or flight for the foot soldiers of the insurgency. Essentially this means a clear route for former insurgents to return to their villages and go back to farming the land or a role for some of them within the legitimate Afghan security forces.'

William Hague, the shadow Foreign Secretary, called for a 'comprehensive strategy' for stabilising Afghanistan. He said: 'It must include clear, tightly drawn, realistic objectives that are regularly reviewed, more rapid development of Afghan security forces and ensuring battlefield gains are swiftly followed by reconstruction.'

ComRes telephoned 1,008 British adults on 24–26 July 2009. Data were weighted by past vote recall. ComRes is a member of the British Polling Council and abides by its rules. Full tables at www.comres.co.uk.

(http://www.independent.co.uk/news/uk/politics 2009-07-28)

In summary

In this chapter we have examined five steps in evaluating arguments and we have applied what we have learnt previously about the key aspects of argument evaluation to a number of exercises. We ended this chapter by introducing you to the margin note and summary method. We pointed out that this method is useful and saves you time when evaluating extended arguments. Evaluating the arguments of other writers is a good way to prepare for the challenging task of constructing your own philosophical arguments. This is the aim of the next chapter.

Constructing arguments and writing argumentative essays

CHAPTER 8

There are no dull subjects. There are only dull writers.

H L Mencken

This chapter focuses on constructing arguments and writing argumentative essays. In the preceding chapters we concentrated on the task of how to *think* critically and how to read, analyse and evaluate the arguments of others. This is only one aspect of critical reasoning. As a critical thinker, you must also know how to express your thoughts *in writing* and this involves knowing how to construct arguments. When you write philosophical essays you must apply the criteria for acceptable arguments to your own arguments.

Writing is difficult and it takes a lot of practice to express one's thoughts and ideas in writing. However, you can learn skills that will help you to be a better writer. You can learn the necessary skills to construct an essay that is coherent, clear and convincing. In this chapter we will look at the process of writing and provide guidelines for writing a good critical essay.

You will find the hints and guidelines for writing a good critical essay, which we discuss here, helpful in some of your other university courses, such as psychology, anthropology, English studies, sociology, political science, teacher education, jurisprudence, and so on. Often, in assignments and examinations, you will come across the instruction to 'discuss critically', 'analyse' and/or 'critically evaluate' an issue, a problem or a statement. Remember that what you have learnt in critical reasoning is not disconnected or divorced from other fields of study; this book will have failed if you do not apply the knowledge and critical skills you have acquired here to your other subjects, and to everyday life (your domestic life, your work situation and your communication and interaction with other people).

1   Different kinds of writing

In chapter 3, I pointed out that critical reasoning is concerned with arguments and argumentation. Therefore, critical reasoning is concerned with *argumentative writing*. You should be aware that argumentative writing is not the only kind of writing. In fact, there are many different forms of writing. Here will we focus on four kinds of writing: descriptive writing, comparative and contrast writing, narrative writing, and argumentative writing. Although critical reasoning's primary focus is argumentative writing, we should also know about other forms of writing, because this will give us a better idea of what argumentative writing is all about.

1.1   Descriptive writing

The aim of *descriptive writing* is to give information and to describe something. Descriptive writing is often very concrete and concentrates on facts, rather than conveying an opinion. Here is an example of descriptive writing:

> Conditions of imprisonment varied from time to time in different places and with different groups. In general there was a shortage, wearisome sameness, and deficiency of food; much physical misery and disease; squalid living conditions; fear and despair; horrible monotony ... inadequate clothing and cleansing facilities; temperature extremes; and physical abuse. (Coleman et al 1984:180)

The author of this passage is describing the effects of imprisonment and the mistreatment of prisoners. Note that he is giving *information* about the conditions of imprisonment. He is not offering his opinion; nor is he engaging in an argument.

1.2   Comparative and contrast writing

The aim of *comparative and contrast writing* is to compare two or more things, events or viewpoints, giving similarities and differences. For example, it might compare two psychological disorders, two authors' perspectives on the notion of personhood, or two perspectives on the notion of human rights. Here is an example of comparison writing:

> Broadly speaking, concerns about human rights presently fall into two schools: liberal and communitarian. Liberals give primary moral value to individual human beings and believe that the individual has autonomy and dignity and therefore should be free to express his or her unique qualities and dispositions and that these should be respected by the community and the state. Liberals base the notion of human rights on the democratic basis of basic civil and political rights of all citizens as individuals and insist that since the individual's interests can easily be threatened, all citizens should be protected against the oppression of the state and against collective authoritarianism.
>
> In contrast to the liberal perspective, communitarians emphasize the value of specifically communal and public goods, and conceive of values as primarily rooted

in communal practices. They argue that the community, rather than the individual, the state, or the nation is the ultimate originator of values and in their analysis of human rights, group or communal rights, rather than individual rights, are emphasized. Thus, according to them, for the survival and the preservation of the community and hence its members' personal lives, it would be perfectly justifiable for some individual rights and acts to be restricted or even banned, especially those rights-claims of individuals whose actions are not in harmony with the ways of society and which are considered a threat to maintaining the 'good' of the community at large. (Van den Berg 1999:194-195)

Note that in the passage above, the author first gives the attributes of a liberal attitude and then goes on to describe a communitarian approach.

1.3 Narrative writing

Narrative writing tells a story or gives a report on something that happened. Novels belong in the category of narrative and aim at unfolding a story or recounting a series of events. Here is an example of narrative writing:

Do you know the story of the Lord of Shorth, who forced the Foretellers of Asen Fastness to answer the question What is the meaning of life? Well, it was a couple of thousand years ago. The Foretellers stayed in the darkness for six days and nights. At the end, all the Celibates were catatonic, the Zanies were dead, the Pervert clubbed the Lord of Shorth to death with a stone, and the Weaver ... . He was a man named Meshe. (Ursula LeGuin 1994:57)

Narrative writing, like the above passage, usually relates events in the order in which they happened.

1.4 Argumentative writing

Argumentative writing is concerned with arguments and the point of an argument is to convince the reader that a claim is true. The aim of argumentative writing is to reason through arguments about an issue that is controversial or open to debate. Argumentative writing argues for or against a particular point of view. *The writing you will be asked to do in critical reasoning is argumentative.* The following is an example of argumentative writing:

He [Max Scheler] generalizes the notion of 'inner perception' (the perception of feelings, for example), which applies as much to other people as to oneself. On the one hand, the perception of my own body or of my own behavior is as external as, and no more immediate than, the perception of objects. On the other hand, we see, we perceive the feelings of others (not only their expression); we perceive them with the same certitude as our own feelings. The differences between the diverse feelings are provided by the perception itself. For example, it is impossible to confuse in other people the redness of shame with that of anger, heated arousal, etc. Perception takes us a long way into the comprehension of other people. There is the perception of the will of others as well; sometimes we even perceive it as our own will, etc. It would be necessary to speak of a 'current of undifferentiated psychic experience', a mixture of self and others, primitive consciousness in a kind of generality, a state of permanent 'hysteria' (in the sense of an indistinctness between that which is lived and that which is only imagined between self and others).

How does the consciousness of self emerge from this indistinctness? Scheler says that one has a consciousness of self only through expression (acts, reactions, etc.) – one takes on consciousness of self as he does of others, in the same way that intentions are only known once they are realized.

Thus, consciousness of self cannot be given a privileged position. It is impossible without consciousness of others. It is of the same variety. Like all experience, the experience of self exists only as a figure against a ground. (Perception of others is like the ground from which perception of self separates itself.) We see ourselves through the intermediary of others. ...

For Max Scheler, consciousness is inseparable from its expression ... There is no radical difference between consciousness of self and consciousness of other people.

But does that make it clear how the subject comes to posit other people? How is there an isolation and a plurality of consciousnesses? (Merleau-Ponty 1991: 45–46)

This text is an example of argumentative writing. The author reasons through arguments about the controversial issue of inner perception and the problem of perceiving or experiencing other people. Since there are different viewpoints on the issue of perception, the problem cannot be solved by employing the strategies of description, narration or comparison.

When constructing argumentative essays you should develop a thesis, stating clearly the point of view you will defend on the issue under discussion, and then offer supporting evidence to convince the reader of your point of view. In the next section we will explore argumentative writing in more detail. I will provide you with helpful guidelines on how to write an argumentative essay.

Exercise

Read the following passages carefully and identify the kind of writing in each text:

1. The day *may* come when the rest of the animal creation may acquire those rights which never could have been withholden from them but by the hand of tyranny. The French have already discovered that the blackness of the skin is no reason why a human being should be abandoned without redress to the caprice of a tormentor. It may one day come to be recognized that the number of the legs, the villosity of the skin, or the termination of the *os sacrum* are reasons equally insufficient for abandoning a sensitive being to the same fate. What else is it that should trace the insuperable line? Is it the faculty of reason, or perhaps the faculty of discourse? But a full-grown horse or dog is beyond comparison a more rational, as well as a more conversable animal, than an infant of a day or a week or even a month, old. But suppose they were otherwise, what would it avail? The question is not, Can they *reason*? nor Can they *talk*? But, *Can they suffer*? (Bentham 1970: 368)

2. Men will curse as they kill, yet accomplish deeds of self-sacrifice, giving their lives for others; poets will write with their pens dipped in blood, yet will write not of death but of life eternal; strong and courteous friendships will be born, to endure in the face of enmity and destruction. And so persistent is this urge to the ideal, above all in the presence of great disaster, that mankind, the wilful destroyer of beauty, must immediately strive to create new beauties, lest it perish from a sense of its own desolation; and this urge touched the Celtic soul of Mary.

   For the Celtic soul is the stronghold of dreams, of longings come down the dim paths of the ages; and within it there dwells a vague discontent, so that it must for ever go questing. And now as though drawn by some hidden attraction, as though stirred by some irresistible impulse, quite beyond the realms of her own understanding, Mary turned in all faith and all innocence to Stephen. (Hall 1985:286)

3. Parental deprivation refers to an absence of adequate care from and interaction with parents or parent-substitutes during the formative years. It can occur even in intact families where, for one reason or another, parents are unable (e.g. because of mental disorder) or unwilling to provide for the child's needs for close and frequent human contact. Its most severe manifestations, however, are usually seen among abandoned or orphaned children who may either be institutionalized or placed in a succession of psychologically unwholesome foster homes. ...

[The] effects of parental deprivation can be extremely serious. Faulty development has often been observed in infants experiencing deprivation. Many studies have focussed on the role of the mother, but all such studies are essentially concerned with warmth and stimulation, whether it comes from the mother, the father, or institutional staff members. (Coleman et al 1984:119)

4. Underlying these two different approaches to the question of African philosophy are two different understandings of philosophy itself. The first emphasizes the universality of philosophical truth and even of philosophical method; the second stresses the fact that actual philosophy is always produced in a particular culture and language and develops particular sets of concepts to deal with particular intellectual problems that are felt to be important. (Shutte 1993:17)

Answers

1. This kind of writing is argumentative. The author does not tell a story, nor does he compare or describe things. The author is engaged in an argument in favour of animal rights.

2. This kind of writing is narrative writing. Note that the text does not argue for or against a particular point of view. Rather, the text aims at *unfolding a story*.

3. This text is an example of descriptive writing. Note that the author is not telling a story, comparing phenomena, or engaging in an argument. The author is *describing* the effects of parental deprivation in children.

4. This kind of writing is comparative writing. Here the author *compares* two different approaches to the question of African philosophy by drawing out the differences between two different understandings of philosophy.

2   Writing an argumentative essay

There is no standard method for writing critical philosophical essays. In studying this book and other philosophical texts you will encounter many styles of philosophical writing and approaches to philosophical issues. Writing critical philosophical essays is a skill that can be improved with practice. The more you read, the better you will understand. And the more you write, the better you will become at it.

When confronted with the task of writing a critical essay for the first time, it is difficult to know where to begin. Here are some guidelines for writing an argumentative essay:

2.1 Statement of the thesis

An argumentative essay involves reasoning or arguing about an issue: you have to take a position. It entails arguing for or against a particular point of view. Philosophical issues are controversial and open to debate. When Bertrand Russell said that philosophy is moved by debate only, he meant that philosophical issues cannot be settled by empirical observation or by describing or comparing events, or by narration, but that philosophy or argumentation involves reasoning through arguments, in which the arguer clearly states the point of view he or she will defend and then supplies acceptable reasons to convince the reader of his or her position.

The first step in constructing an argumentative essay, then, is to state clearly what the thesis of the argument is. The *thesis* of your argument is a *clear statement of the position you will defend*. Supposing your topic deals with the problem of euthanasia. You decide to defend the position that active voluntary euthanasia is morally justifiable. A statement of your thesis may be the following: 'Active voluntary euthanasia can be defended on the moral ground that each individual has a right to personal dignity and autonomy and this right includes the right to decide over the time and manner of one's death'. Whatever you write down as the thesis is the point of view you will defend in your essay. Try to express the thesis in a single, clear sentence.

Keep in mind that your thesis must follow logically from the reasons you intend to give in support of it. Also keep in mind that an argumentative essay consists of a series of arguments that must be substantiated by sufficient reasons. So do not start your thesis with expressions such as 'I feel that ...', 'I believe ...', 'The Bible says ...', or 'God says that ...'

> **Note:** An argumentative essay is not a narration of your religious convictions or feelings. These are matters of faith. Critical philosophical arguments, on the other hand, involve supporting a point of view on rational grounds. Of course, you may put forward an argument in favour of atheism ('God does not exist') or theism ('God exists'), but then you have to support your argument with reasons.

2.2 Use research material, documentation and referencing

Doing research into the topic you are writing about and *using research material* appropriately in your essay is essential to critical or argumentative essay writing. You need to consult sources to collect evidence and support for the claims you make on the issue you are dealing with. In other words, we do research to learn more about writing; to supplement, examine, verify and often modify our own ideas on the topic; and to find support for our arguments. Research should never be an attempt to substitute another thinker's ideas for your own. That is why it is important always to give credit for *any ideas and views that are not your own*. If you quote, paraphrase or borrow an idea from someone, use references and give credit. The failure to credit sources is called plagiarism. In the academic world this is considered a serious offence, because plagiarism is a form of intellectual dishonesty (claiming another's work as your own).

The purpose of *referencing* is to distinguish between the parts of your essay that are your ideas and the parts that are other people's ideas. Other authors' and thinkers' ideas, viewpoints and words do not belong to you and should therefore be referenced so that your reader knows where they come from. Keep in mind that, even when you are paraphrasing – mentioning someone else's views indirectly – you need to give the author's name in your text and you need to include the name in your list of references.

To enable you to refer to an author's work or ideas, it is important to *document research sources* as you proceed. This means that you should write down the details of each text you use as you take notes and write the drafts of your essay. Failure to do this will cost you extra time, because you will have to go back to all the sources you have consulted and page through them at length in an attempt to find specific quotations. This is an unnecessary waste of time. An even worse scenario is that you do not have enough time left to trace the sources you have used. There is little value in an accomplished piece of work if the references, footnotes and bibliography are missing.

Remember to *include a bibliography* or list of the sources you have consulted at the end of your assignment, essay or paper. Very few people know so much about a topic that they do not need to draw on other experts' views and academic sources. A bibliography mentions all the sources (articles, books, newspapers, internet sites, study guides and so on) that you have consulted and referred to in your essay. For more information on referencing and compiling a bibliography, consult *Reference techniques* by Marlene Burger (see bibliography for details).

2.3 *Provide sufficient reasons to support the thesis*

After you have clearly stated the point of view you will defend, you have to argue your claim to convince the reader of your position. Convincing the reader of your point of view means you must *give good reasons* for accepting the premises of your argument and the premises must *support the conclusion*. The reasons you offer in support of your claim must be *relevant*. Every point must be *directly related* to your thesis. Stay on track and do not wander onto side paths, pursuing issues that have little or no relevance to your topic and the aims of your essay. A good way of checking this is to go back to the introduction after you have written a complete draft and see if your essay has done what you proposed in the introduction. Do not enter into a general discussion, but refer only to those issues and arguments that are relevant to the question at hand and discuss these issues and arguments critically. For example, if you construct a philosophical argument on euthanasia, *do not* discuss euthanasia in *general*. Instead, state clearly which type of euthanasia your argument addresses. If you have decided to write a philosophical argument on the ethical justification of, for example, active voluntary euthanasia, then refer only to those issues and arguments that are relevant to active voluntary euthanasia.

Examine your work for weak arguments and poorly articulated points and correct them by structuring your arguments more logically and by expressing your points more clearly and persuasively. Note that writing persuasively does *not* mean you must 'decorate' your writing by using more complicated terms or language. Take care that you provide enough support for all your claims. Check that all the paragraphs in the body of your essay build on one another. This means that each paragraph should be connected to the next paragraph: do not jump from one train of thought to another, but link your arguments together. Another point to remember is to connect your quotes and examples: do not let them hang 'in space'. A good quote is very effective, but you have to link it to the argument you are advancing and it must be relevant to the point you are making. The purpose of using quotes and examples is to illustrate or illuminate your ideas to strengthen your arguments.

2.4 Define key concepts

When constructing philosophical arguments it is important to *explain the key terminology* and to *define the key concepts* you are using because, often, the plausibility of arguments depends on how successfully you have explicated the concepts you use. You should define terms right at the beginning of your essay to avoid misunderstanding and confusion. When using abstract and ambiguous terms that are open to interpretation, such as 'person', 'equality', 'abortion', 'affirmative action', 'euthanasia', 'xenophobia' or 'social responsibility', it is crucial to explain what you mean by these concepts. You cannot take for granted that your reader will have the same understanding as you do of these ambiguous concepts. In chapter 5, I explained the importance of definitions when evaluating arguments and writing argumentative essays of your own.

2.5 Consider possible counterarguments

Always consider possible objections to your position. If we assume that many readers think for themselves, then we can be sure that they will ask critical questions about the cogency and acceptability of the claims we make in our arguments. So, be prepared to defend your thesis by *anticipating possible counterarguments.* Here you can pretend that you are an outside person or a critical reader of your essay who objects to your position. Imagine what arguments this person could use against your thesis to defeat it. Then reply to the counterarguments by showing that you have supplied strong evidence in support of your argument. If your critical reader's objections hold, then you have to examine your essay very carefully for bad arguments and reformulate your points more clearly and cogently. In chapter 5 we discussed the role of counterexamples and counterarguments and I pointed out that the use of counterarguments is a helpful way of testing the plausibility of arguments. If you have forgotten this aspect of argumentation, return to chapter 5 to refresh your memory.

2.6 *Use appropriate language*

Avoid using prejudiced language or 'loaded' terms. For instance, do not make judgements such as 'stupid', 'idiotic', 'absurd', 'senseless', 'ridiculous' and so on, unless you can give evidence confirming your judgement to be well-founded. However, it is better to *refrain from using heavy-handed or emotional language.* Try to make your point with a carefully reasoned argument instead of relying on emotional terms.

Discriminatory and gendered language use must be avoided, because it is unjustified and unacceptable. Some authors state at the beginning of their essays or articles that the use of the term 'man' should be understood as neutral, referring to 'human beings' in general, and that the same applies to the use of the terms 'he', 'his' and 'him', which usually denote the male gender. They think that they are covered by making this kind of statement, but later on in the text they lapse into sexist language use with terms such as 'brotherhood' (meaning humankind) and 'men' (meaning human beings). This kind of language has the effect of excluding women. Consider the following example, quoted from a thesis: 'In my analysis of the Sartrean concept *for-itself,* I will consider the *for-itself* as being a human being, a human reality or simply a man.' The question that arises is, 'does the *for-itself* then not apply to women?'

What good is it to claim that one is gender-sensitive and culture-sensitive if one easily lapses into discriminatory and sexist language use? The use of *discriminatory and sexist language is never justified,* because it perpetuates sexism and exclusiveness.

Critical reasoning involves far more than just analysing and evaluating the arguments of other people. As a critical thinker you must be able to express your thoughts effectively and clearly in *writing* and construct arguments of your own that meet the accepted standards of good arguments.

Exercise

Write an argumentative essay on a topic of your choice. Your essay need not be more than 2 000 words. You could also consider writing on one of the following topics.

1. Is xenophobia justifiable?
2. Is the death penalty morally justifiable?
3. Consider arguments for and against affirmative action and give your own opinion on the justifiability of affirmative action.
4. Do animals have rights? Discuss critically.
5. Write a critical essay on sexual harassment, in which you express your informed opinion on the problem.
6. Write a critical essay on the ethics of health care, in which you express an informed opinion on the problem of the equal distribution of healthcare resources between the rich and the poor.

In summary

In this book you have accompanied me on a journey of critical reasoning. Along the way we explored a number of important aspects of critical reasoning. We examined obstacles to clear thinking and noted why it is important to avoid them. We engaged in analysing arguments and explored the meaning of texts by evaluating arguments. Finally, we discussed argumentative essay writing and you practised constructing your own critical philosophical arguments.

A journey in critical reasoning is, however, not complete until we dare to travel the path of self-discovery and critical self-reflection. We will not be able to acquire a critical attitude or critically evaluate the ideas and beliefs of other people unless we adopt an attitude of self-reflection and critical evaluation of *our own* biases, impediments to thinking, misconceptions and preconceived ideas. I believe firmly that critical reasoning is empty without adopting an attitude of critical *self-*reflection. By critical self-reflection I mean the ability to first reflect critically on our own assumptions, motives, deceptions, beliefs, preconceived ideas, prejudicial biases and attitudes before you judge the ideas, beliefs, worldviews, attitudes and arguments of others. It is easy to criticise others' thoughts, ideas and actions, but it is difficult, even painful, to subject our own thoughts, ideas and motives to critical scrutiny. Critical reasoning is an adventure that demands hard work, intellectual rigour, fairness and honesty. Knowledge and skills are empty without wisdom. Wisdom is a critical philosophical attitude, a state of being, of critical self-reflection, in fact.

3   Reflection

At the beginning of this book, in chapter 1, I asked you to write down a definition of critical reasoning. At that stage we had only started our journey of critical reasoning and perhaps you only had a narrow understanding of what critical reasoning entails. Now that you have progressed through this book you should have a much clearer idea of what critical reasoning is all about. Take the time and trouble to reflect on your journey of critical thinking. Now write down your own definition of critical reasoning by drawing on the insights and critical competence that you have gained from exploring this text on critical reasoning. Ask yourself the following questions: 'Have my preconceived ideas been challenged?' 'How did critical reasoning help me to become aware of my wrong-headed beliefs?' 'How has critical reasoning changed my perception of the world, other people and myself?' 'Have I acquired the basic competency to *think for myself*, that is, to critically question, analyse, interpret and evaluate the ideas and beliefs of others in the light of the reasons offered in support of their claims?' 'Have I developed a critical attitude of *critical self-reflection*? In other words, do I critically question the assumptions, biases and preconceived ideas on which my claims are based?' 'Have I acquired the basic competency to *reason in an informed way*? Differently put, do I give reasons or evidence in support of my beliefs and claims?'

References

Andolina, M. 2002. *Practical guide to critical thinking*. Albany, NY: Delmar.

Bentham, J. 1970. *Introduction to the principles of morals and legislation*. London: Athlone.

BootsnAll Travel Articles. South Africa race relations – South Africa. http://www. bootsnall.com/articles/05-11/south-africa-race-relations-south-africa.html. Accessed on 30 July 2009.

Brookfield, SD. 1987. *Developing critical thinkers: challenging adults to explore alternative ways of thinking and acting*. San Francisco: Jossey-Bass.

Burger, M. 1992. *Reference techniques*. Pretoria: Unisa Press.

Cederblom, J & Paulsen, DW. 2001. *Critical reasoning*. London: Wadsworth.

Chaffee, J. 1992. Critical thinking skills: the cornerstone of development education. *Journal of Development Education* 15(3):2–39.

Coleman, JC, Butcher, JN & Carson, RC. 1984. *Abnormal psychology and modern life*. Glenview, Ill: Scott.

Descartes, R. 1986. *Meditations on first philosophy*. Translated by John Cottingham. Cambridge: Cambridge University Press.

Economist.com. Going nowhere: Zimbabwe will only recover when Robert Mugabe goes. http://www.economist.com/daily/news/newsprint.cfm?story 2/21/2007 9:39:49 AM. Accessed on 30 July 2009.

Elder, L & Paul, R. 1994. Critical thinking: why we must transform our teaching. *Journal of Developmental Education* 18(1):31–40.

Epstein, RL. 1999. *Critical thinking*. London: Wadsworth.

Fisher, A. 2001. *Critical thinking: an introduction*. Cambridge: University Press.

Fletcher, W. 1978. *Advertising*. London: Hodder and Stoughton.

Freeley, AJ. 1993. *Argumentation and debate*. Belmont, Calif: Wadsworth.

Freeman, SJ. 1999. *Ethics: An introduction to philosophy and practice*. Belmont, CA: Wadsworth.

Hall, R. 1985. *The well of loneliness*. London: Virago.

Halpern, DF. 1989. *Thought and knowledge: an introduction to critical thinking*. Hillsdale, NJ: Erlbaum.

Herman, AL. 1976. *An introduction to Indian thought*. Englewood-Cliffs, NJ: Prentice Hall.

Horner, C & Westacott, E. 2000. *Thinking through philosophy*. Cambridge: University Press.

Hospers, J. 1970. *An introduction to philosophical analysis*. Englewood Cliffs, NJ: Prentice Hall.

Independent Online. Court put on hold hearing on Zuma charges. http://www.iol.co.za/general/news/newsprint.php?art 2009-06-09 17:09:49. Accessed on 30 July 2009.

Instablogs. Dafur crimes against humanity and international failure. http://liberator.instablogs.com/entry/darfur-crimes-against-humanity-and-internationa-failure Dec 9 2008. Accessed on 30 July 2009.

Kahane, H & Cavender, N. 2006. *Logic and contemporary rhetoric*. Belmont, Calif: Wadsworth.

LeGuin, U. 1994. *The left hand of darkness*. London: Orbit.

Karrim, Q. 2009. Local leaders 'behind xenophobic attacks'. *Mail & Guardian*, March 11: 56.

Marx, K. 1936. *The poverty of philosophy*. London: Lawrence & Wishart.

Marx, K & Engels, F. 1998. *The communist manifesto*. London: Verso.

Merleau-Ponty, M. 1991. *Consciousness and the acquisition of language*. Translated by Hugh J Silverman. Evanston, Ill: Northwestern University Press.

Morton, A. 1996. *Philosophy in practice*. Oxford: Blackwell.

Olen, J & Barry, V. 1999. *Applying ethics*. 7th edition. New York: Wadsworth.

Olen, J, Van Camp, JC & Barry, V. 2005. *Applying ethics*. 8th edition. Belmont, MA: Wadsworth/Thomson Learning.

Paul, RW. 1993. The logic of creative and critical thinking. *American Behavioral Scientist* 37(1):21–40.

Plato. 1923. *The Republic*. Translated into English by AD Lindsay. London: Dent.

Plato, 1961. *The last days of Socrates*. Translated and with an introduction by Hugh Tredennick. Harmondsworth: Penguin.

Schopenhauer, A. 1969. *The world as will and representation*, vol 1. New York: Dover.

Shutte, A. 1993. *Philosophy for Africa*. Rondebosch: UCT Press.

Sogolo, G. 1993. *Foundations of African philosophy*. Nigeria: Ibadan University Press.

Teays, W. 1996. *Critical thinking from a multicultural perspective*. Mountain View, CA.: Mayfield.

Teays, W. 2003. *Second thoughts: critical thinking for a diverse society*. New York: McGraw-Hill.

The Independent. Voters turn against war in Afghanistan. http://www.independent.co.uk/news/uk/politics/voters-turn-against-war-in-afghanistan 28 July 2009. Accessed on 30 July 2009.

Thomson, JJ. 1999. A defense of abortion, in *Applying ethics*, edited by J Olen & V Barry. New York: Wadsworth: 187–198.

Van den Berg, MES. 1999. On a communitarian ethos, equality and human rights in Africa. *Alternation* 6(1): 193–212.

Wolff, RP. 1986. *About philosophy*. Englewood Cliffs, NJ: Prentice-Hall.

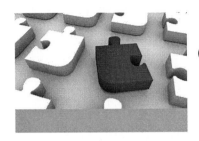

Glossary

***Ad hominem* argument.** This type of fallacy occurs when someone makes a personal attack on the character, interests or circumstances of the person who is advancing a claim, instead of addressing the argument he or she makes.

Affirming the consequent. This fallacy is committed when the consequent in a conditional statement is affirmed and the antecedent is taken to be true on these grounds.

Analogy. Reasoning by analogy is based on comparison with similar cases. An argument based on analogy only succeeds when the similarities between the cases or entities are relevant.

Analysing arguments. The process of identifying premises and conclusions in arguments and structuring arguments.

Antecedent. In a conditional claim ('if...then...') the antecedent lies between the 'if' and the 'then'. An antecedent is the condition that is claimed to lead to the consequent.

Appeal to force. The appeal-to-force fallacy occurs when an arguer appeals to the threat of force or coercion in order to get his or her opponents to accept a certain conclusion.

Appeal to the masses. Fallacious reasoning based on mass sentiment, popular feelings, or nationalism, rather than offering good reasons for accepting a conclusion.

Argument. An argument is a group of statements that intend to affirm the truth or acceptability of a claim.

Argumentative writing. Argumentative writing argues for or against a particular point of view. It is concerned with arguments and the point of an argument is to convince the reader or the audience that a claim is true or acceptable.

Begging the question fallacy. This fallacy occurs when the premises of an argument assume the very issue that the conclusion needs to establish. The begging-the-question fallacy is also known as circular reasoning because the 'reasoning' goes round in a circle, that is, it only restates the premises in different words.

Cause-and-effect reasoning. A kind of inductive argument in which it is argued that a particular event or effect occurs on the basis of specific antecedent conditions or causal factors.

Comparison writing. A kind of writing that compares or contrasts two or more things, events or viewpoints by focusing on similarities and differences.

Complex question. The complex-question fallacy occurs when two or more questions are combined and demand a 'yes' or 'no' answer.

Conclusion indicator. A signal word that helps us to identify the conclusion of an argument.

Conclusion. A conclusion is the main claim of an argument.

Conditional claim. A conditional claim is a proposition that can be expressed in the form of 'If P then Q', where P and Q stand for statements. It is called a conditional claim because the antecedent (the statement that follows after the 'if') may not be true.

Consequent. In a conditional claim ('if…then…') the consequent follows the 'then'. A consequent is what is said to follow if the antecedent condition is assumed to be true.

Counterargument. This is an argument an arguer formulates in answer to another argument.

Counterexample. A counterexample is a specific example which defeats or runs counter to the claim made in an argument.

Critical reasoning. Critical reasoning explores the nature and function of arguments in natural language and is concerned with the art of argumentation rather than the formal theory of reasoning. Critical reasoning involves thinking for yourself, offering well-informed and reasoned alternatives to problems, and an attitude of critical self-reflection, that is, the ability to reflect critically on your own beliefs and biases and the beliefs and biases of other people.

Deductive argument. An argument in which the premises are claimed to give sufficient support for the conclusion to follow.

Denotative definition. A definition that denotes or 'marks down' by giving examples. A denotative definition is also called a definition by example.

Denying the antecedent. This type of fallacy occurs when someone argues that because the antecedent doesn't happen, the consequent cannot happen. In a conditional claim it is fallacious to deny the antecedent and to assume that this is a ground for denying the consequent.

Descriptive writing. A kind of writing that describes something or gives information about a state of affairs or events.

Distraction fallacies. These fallacies occur when attention is distracted from the weak point of an argument. The fallacious argument appears to be sound because of a false link to an argument that really is sound. Distraction fallacies include slippery slope, straw man, begging the question, equivocation, complex question and faulty analogy.

Emotion fallacies. These fallacies confuse emotion with reason. They contain flaws in reasoning because of their illegitimate appeal to emotion. Emotion fallacies include *ad hominem* arguments, false appeal to authority, appeal to force, appeal to the masses, false dilemma and hasty generalisation.

Empirical argument. An argument in which the premises assert that some empirically determinable facts apply.

Equivocation. The fallacy of equivocation occurs when a word or phrase shifts meaning from one premise to another and leads to an incorrect conclusion.

Evaluating arguments. The process of critically examining the plausibility of claims advanced in an argument; critically considering assumptions, preconceived ideas and fallacious reasoning; weighing possible solutions to issues; making informed and reasoned decisions; forming one's own opinion on issues; and locating issues within a global perspective.

Fallacy. A fallacy is a misleading argument that tries to persuade us, but is unsound because it is not supported by evidence or reasoned argumentation. All fallacies contain fundamental flaws in reasoning. The flaws may entail distraction, or emotional or structural errors in reasoning.

False appeal to authority. This fallacy is committed when someone cites an authoritative or famous person who is not an expert in the field under discussion.

False dilemma. A false dilemma is created when an arguer presents an either–or choice when, in fact, there are more alternatives.

Faulty analogy. This fallacy occurs when a comparison is drawn between two different cases or issues, and there are no relevant similarities between them.

Formal logic. Formal logic examines the formal structure of arguments in logical language or symbols and it employs precise rules for testing the validity of arguments.

Hasty generalisation. The fallacy of generalisation occurs when a conclusion is drawn on the basis of ill-considered or insufficient evidence.

Inductive argument. An argument in which the conclusion is subject to probability, even if the premises are assumed to be true.

Logical definition. This type of definition defines a term by selecting those properties that are shared by, and confined to, all the things that the term covers.

Modus ponens. A valid deductive argument of the form: If P, then S. P. Therefore S.

Modus tollens. A valid deductive argument of the form: If P, then S. Not S. Therefore not P.

Narrative writing. This kind of writing aims at unfolding a story or recounting a series of events.

Persuasive definition. This type of definition aims at influencing the reader's attitude and thinking by suggesting a new meaning for a term that is already in common use.

Preconceived idea. A preconceived idea is a societal assumption that is not supported by reasoned argument and evidence.

Premise indicator. Premise indicators are signal words that help us to identify the premises in an argument.

Premise. A premise is a statement that is suppose to serve as a reason for accepting the conclusion in an argument.

Principle of charitable interpretation. This principle entails that, when more than one interpretation of an argument is possible, the argument should be interpreted so that the premises provide the strongest support for the conclusion.

Slippery slope argument. A slippery slope argument entails reasoning in a chain with conditionals (*if* so, *then* something else), where at least one of the if–then premises is false or doubtful and the conclusion does not follow.

Soundness. Soundness refers to the truth or strength of the premises of an argument.

Statement. A statement is an assertion that is either true or false. Note that questions, exclamations, requests and commands are not statements and they can be neither true nor false.

Statistical extrapolation. A kind of inductive reasoning that refers to some statistical study or evidence. An inference is drawn about a target population on the basis of what is taken to be true of a sample group.

Stipulative definition. A definition that stipulates or suggests that a given term should be used in a particular way. It is also called a coining definition because it 'coins' or assigns meaning to a new term.

Straw man argument. This fallacy consists of making one's own position appear strong by ridiculing the opposition's argument.

Structural fallacies. These fallacies contain flaws in reasoning because their form or structure is not valid. They *appear* to be valid because of a counterfeit resemblance to the form or structure of a valid argument. Structural fallacies include affirming the consequent and denying the antecedent.

Validity. Validity refers to the relationship between the premises and the conclusion of an argument.

Value argument. An argument that asserts a judgement of a moral claim about what one ought or ought not do.

Index